INDU

"I HATE this book. Rob's vulnerability with his failures and losses made me rethink my entire life. Was I acting like a Victim or a Conqueror? If you want to challenge everything you think you are to get a better result, then read and apply this book."

WOODY WOODWARD
CEO Renegade Sales Academy
Sales Trainer - Author - Professional Speaker

"This book is an important conversation about the mindsets and the fears that hold us back. As entrepreneurs, this is a conversation that is crucial to your success. Rob does a masterful job of addressing these complex ideas and making them simple, real, and actionable. I highly recommend this book!"

TY BENNETT
Author of *The Power of Storytelling*

"Rob Sperry does it again! This is a profound work of art. It is raw, rare and remarkable in it's storytelling and education. Rob is a student of success, a student of life, and a student of network marketing leadership. The Fears on which he shines light will set you free."

RICHARD BLISS BROOKE
Author and Ontological Coach
The Four Year Career, Mach 2 and The Authentic Networker

"When Rob asked me to write a testimonial for his new book, it was at an exceptionally busy time of year and at the same time I was leaving on a 2 week journey through Europe. My first thought was, "I don't really have the time right now to read the book and write a review!" I started skimming the first chapter and I found it riveting and raw. The first few paragraphs hooked me and I couldn't put it down. A tragic set of circumstances that Rob and his family endured lays out the framework for some great business and life lessons.

Also, because Rob is the founder of one of the largest online groups of network marketing leaders ever assembled, he owns a perspective that helps him to see the patterns of behavior that drive success and failure in our business. Fears are the #1 enemy to success in business and Rob digs deep on how it drives you and what you can do about it.

This book possesses great value for the aspiring network marketer or even the seasoned leader that needs to develop and train a team. Thank you Rob for coming out with another great book!"

JORDAN ADLER
Author of the Amazon Best Seller, *Beach Money*
Network Marketing Millionaire

"Well, my intention was to skim it but I just got sucked into it and couldn't stop reading it! IT IS AWESOME!!!!

The Game of Conquering should hands down be the very first book any network marketer should pick up if they truly want to crush it. As Rob shares, most of us are focused on not quitting instead of winning. What if you were given all the practical tools necessary to tackle every area of inadequacy we all experience at one time or another? Rob will literally teach you how to shift into a conqueror mindset. Grab this book so you can light up your biz!"

KIMBERLY OLSON
Best Selling Author, Speaker & Podcast Hostess

"Rob has done it again! His level of transparency in this book is what network marketers need to hear today. Being entrepreneurs, we all face adversity, feeling like the victim, and have overwhelming fears. In this book, *The Game of Conquering*, Rob has broken it down so simple on how you can OVERCOME them to help create even more success in YOUR life and business as he shares some of his most intimate stories.

I have so much respect and admiration for Rob as he shares his struggles in this book to help inspire you, the reader. His perspective will have you thinking, shifting your mindset immediately and ultimately conquering these things to make you a better person and leader in network marketing."

BRIAN FRYER
Coach, Social Media Strategist, and Speaker

"Since I began my journey in Network Marketing in 1982, I have been in the presence of some of the real giants. Today my list is very short on who I have total trust in when it comes to guiding you down the MLM road—Rob Sperry is at the top of that list. A principle centered individual with an abundance of wisdom to share! I was riveted from the opening story in the book."

DAN MCCORMICK
35-year Industry Leader
Multi-million Dollar Earner
Co-Author of *Lessons from Great Lives*

"Rob is a game changer for the Network Marketing profession. Having seen him share his message in a bunch of countries, what he is sharing is so needed and making a huge impact!"

FRAZER BROOKES
Generic Network Marketing Speaker, Coach & Trainer

"*The Game of Conquering* is the BEST book I've read this year, hands down. Your mindset is the #1 thing that determines your success in network marketing and Rob is the perfect one to mold us all into having a winning mindset. How you SHOW up as an entrepreneur, GIVE more, LOVE more and GROW into having a Conqueror mindset determines the impact you will make on this world. SHARE this book with your team ASAP and thank me later. Thank you, Rob for being the ultimate servant leader. Seeing the need for this book in our profession, and delivering in the most incredible way."

DR. DANA MCGRADY
Top Network Marketing Leader
Author of *Magnetic Soulpreneur*

"I believe your mindset and attitude determines 95% of your success and that's why this is a must-read for every network marketer. Most distributors get it wrong; they think it's the technical and how to's. They think it's the magical words you have to say to prospects or the specific number of messages you have to send out to someone before you invite them, or the special filter on Instagram that will create success.

Don't get me wrong—skills are important—but NONE of the skills matter if your mindset and attitude are off track. Rob Sperry does an EXCELLENT job in teaching what it takes to be successful in a fun and easy to read book. I applaud him for being vulnerable and sharing the personal tragedies in his life and how it helped mold him into who he is.

Rob has done tremendous things for the network marketing profession and he steps up once again with this must-read book."

SIMON CHAN
Coach, Speaker and Founder of MLM Nation

"This is a GREAT read for any network marketer … especially for those who have gone through challenges and hit major roadblocks. Rob shares from the heart on how he overcame major life obstacles to achieve success in this profession. It's crazy how sometimes we look at successful people and think they've never had to deal with heavy stuff in their lives. This is a book about overcoming challenges. Read it!"

TODD FALCONE
Network Marketing Trainer and Author of *Fearless Networking*

"If you want to truly help people you have to show them the reality of the journey to success. Don't just show them the highs. Don't shy away from the truth, the fear and the doubt. It's only when a leader tells the truth that they can help them conquer all of the challenges that being successful in our industry will take. The network marketing industry has never had anyone more truthfully approach these topics like Rob Sperry has in this book. It's like arming yourself with the mental tools that you will need as you set out to succeed at the highest level in Network Marketing."

KYLE KIRSCHBAUM
10-year Network Marketing Professional

"Rob is one of the few people in the network marketing profession that not only built a 7-figure business, but also is a phenomenal coach helping others do the same. That's a rare combination. What I love the most about Rob though is his passion and heart for this profession and helping others succeed.

If you are serious about taking your business and life to the next level, and looking for the inspiration and actionable steps to help you do that, this book is a must read."

BOB HELIG
Author, Speaker, and World Renown Leadership Trainer

"Rob's candor and vulnerability matched with his digestible, transforming content makes him one of the premier coaches and trainers of our great profession. Hearing him break down the core attributes of a success mindset will not only inspire a great change in you, but inside of your budding Network Marketing business as well. It takes a brave person to review their faults, their fears, and their successes with abandon. Let Rob lead you on a path to personal victory and you won't go wrong!"

RACHEL JACKSON
Social Influencer and Philanthropist

"Right from the first chapter, you will feel Rob's heart and know that this book is not a bunch of fluff and hype. He has an incredible ability to make you have a dead stop, reflect on your life, hold up a mirror, deal with it, and have a breakthrough all in 5 minutes! His style of writing is so simple for the reader to grasp and his raw authentic teachings will inspire you to step out and into who you were made to really become. We love this book for us, but also for our team!"

SARAH AND TONY ZOLECKI
7-Figure Earners, Top Network Marketing Leaders

"Everyone wants to win at life but most people let their fears overtake them. In this book Rob breaks it down how to conquer your fears so that you can take action towards building and living the life of your dreams. I appreciated his raw honesty of what it really takes in network marketing."

EMILY VAVRA
7 Figure Network Marketing Leader

GO TO WWW.SPERRYBONUS.COM

FOR FREE TRAININGS.

A few of those trainings are:

- The Income Producing Activities

- Your Daily Method of Operation

- The Conqueror's Formula

- Public Speaking Tips

- Free eBook: *From One to a Thousand*

THE
GAME OF
CONQUERING

STRATEGIES TO OVERCOME
FEARS IN NETWORK MARKETING

ROB SPERRY

TGON Publishing

TGON Publishing

Warning—Disclaimer

The purpose of this book is to educate and inspire. This book is not intended to give advice or make promises or guarantees that anyone following the ideas, tips, suggestions, techniques or strategies will have the same results as the people listed throughout the stories contained herein. The author, publisher and distributor(s) shall have neither liability nor responsibility to anyone with respect to any loss or damage caused, or alleged to be caused, directly or indirectly by the information contained in this book.

ISBN 978-1-7343817-0-2

To my best buddy Danny.

CONTENTS

THE GAME OF CONQUERING

"There is no greater agony than bearing an untold story inside you."

-Maya Angelou

INTRODUCTION

We don't talk about our personal experiences enough. Many people feel too vulnerable to share their most challenging experiences. I am no exception.

I spend most of the year traveling the world, speaking to thousands of people. In the past, I rarely would share the experiences in my life that have left me feeling broken and vulnerable. There is risk in sharing with others. I haven't wanted to risk showing emotion, being seen as weak, or being called broken. I call it a risk, but it's really fear.

Fear has held me back from sharing the most personal experiences of my life- and stopped me from connecting with others on a deeper level. You have to practice what you preach—and I am no exception! In telling my stories in this book, my intent is to connect with you and help show you how your own fears, and the mindset they create, are holding you back in life and in network marketing.

In my first book, *The Game of Networking*, I shared 3.5 laws to help increase the skills to build your business and build a referral engine. In this book, I will show you how to overcome your fears and become a CONQUEROR in your network marketing business. I will help you see how being a victim has stopped you from recruiting and sponsoring more. I will help you to become a better leader by teaching you the conqueror's mindset.

I will peel back many layers of fears that you may have not even known existed. Fears that you weren't consciously aware of that have held you back from becoming the BOLD VERSION of YOU. I will help you become the conqueror that you are meant to be in your business.

The events that happen in our lives can never be changed, but how we SEE and REACT TO our own story is what shapes us. We can be victims or survivors of these experiences, OR we can find ways to become conquerors of them. Can you be a conqueror of the most challenging, tragic experiences? We can be victims, survivors, or conquerors of ALL the experiences we have in our lives.

The stories I share in this book have shaped my character, enriched my life, and helped me create success in network marketing. I have been the victim, survivor, and conqueror throughout my life. Sometimes, I have been all three within the same experience. Part of the human experience is failing and working through trying ordeals. My intent for writing this book is to create a place to talk about experiences so that true learning, connection, and growth can happen. It is time for me to become vulnerable and share these stories.

I want to challenge you to do the same thing as you read this book. As I share my stories, I want you to take the time to write down your own stories. What experiences have you had in your own life where you have identified as a victim, survivor, and conqueror? Use this book to learn about these three different mindsets AND as a personal log of your own stories.

Some of the best learning for me has happened while facing my fears. Do you have any fears? I have plenty! As I look at my biggest fears, I have found that they can really be grouped into five different categories of fear. Now, this book isn't going to go into a detailed explanation of fears such as "going to the dentist" or "fear of spiders." But I believe that most, if not ALL, fears can be put into these five categories.

I realized I either gave into the fear or overcame the fear. I then used my experiences to learn and gain insight into myself and my thoughts. I learned the key to this was understanding my mindset. It made all the difference! Because, it's not just the experiences that have been life changing. It's how I have been able to intentionally work through the experiences and reflect on them with the mindset of a conqueror that have made the greatest impact.

"Tragedy should be utilized as a source of strength."

-Tibetan proverb

CHAPTER 1

THE NIGHT WE LOST DANNY

It was 1997, and my parents owned an embroidery business. They would frequently make a ten-hour drive from Utah to California to deliver the orders in a big white cargo van.

My dad was making the drive back to Utah, after dropping off an order in California, to pick up the family for a tennis tournament, which was being held back in California. He had already driven twenty hours and was exhausted, but we were anxious to get on the road. We loaded my dad, myself, my two younger brothers Danny and Mike, and my younger sister Tiff, into the already full cargo van, and started the ten-hour road trip. My mom stayed home because the family business couldn't operate without her being there.

My dad drove, my ten-year-old brother, Danny sat in the front seat, and I was sprawled out comfortably in the back—well, as comfortably as you can be in a packed van—in a sleeping bag, with no seat belt. Not smart, right? Mike laid out next to me and Tiff was beside him. The rest of the van was filled with boxes packed all the way to the top.

At just past the halfway point in our journey, we were an hour or so outside of Las Vegas driving towards a town called Barstow. It was around midnight, and my dad turned to me and said, "Rob, will you drive?"

I didn't care that my dad had just made this trip by himself and had little to no sleep. I was just a self-absorbed teenager who wanted to sleep. I looked at him and said, "Dad—I've got a tournament. I've got to rest. I'm exhausted… I'm tired…"

My dad said, "Okay, that's fine. You rest, Son."

My dad turned to Danny and said, "Hey, Danny, why don't you lay between the two seats so you can sleep." My brother took off his seatbelt and laid down. Then, all of us kids fell asleep.

My dad continued to drive while the rest of us were fast asleep. I had no idea of his struggle as he silently drove through the darkness. He knew this drive very well. He knew all the rest stops along the highway. He was completely exhausted and wanted to pull off at the nearest rest stop, but he was so tired. He lost focus and missed the stop. The next rest stop was approximately 30 miles down the highway.

We never made it there.

My dad fell asleep.

As my dad drifted to sleep, the car drifted too. Just a few seconds, but that was all it took. The tires started driving over the rumble strips on the shoulder of the road. You know what I'm talking about, right? Rumble strips are those ridges at the side of the road that warn drivers of potential danger when they drift too close to the shoulder. My dad snapped awake and quickly over-corrected. The terrible pounding sound of the rumble strips—which sounded eerily like a heartbeat— could be heard again as we veered to the other side of the road.

It was 2 o'clock in the morning. I woke up to what sounded like my own heart beating, and watched my dad make a quick correction to try to get back onto the road. That's when the van rolled.

The van ended up rolling eleven times…

Eleven times—and no seatbelts…

On the second to last roll, Danny fell out the passenger side window. The van rolled right over the top of him. It broke one of his ribs and punctured his lung. He died instantly.

The accident happened so quickly. The physical pain for me came in a flash, and I remember feeling like it was the end.

When the van stopped rolling, I was still lying inside of it, trying to take in what had just happened. I heard my dad say, "Hey, is everyone okay?"

I responded first: "Yeah, I'm okay."

Mike answered, "I'm okay."

Tiff said, "I'm okay."

Then silence.

We didn't hear anything from Danny. We panicked, thinking maybe he was knocked out somewhere. My dad, with only his socks on, kicked out the windshield and crawled out to search for Danny.

My dad found Danny lying in the road, looking up with his arms stretched out and eyes looking toward heaven. My dad touched his eyelids and closed them.

When my siblings and I crawled out of the car, my mind couldn't process what I saw. Between the physical pain, the shock of the event, and finding my dad with Danny, it was all too much for my sixteen-year-old self to handle. I kept telling myself that Danny couldn't be dead. That kind of stuff just didn't happen. Or at least it didn't happen to me—to my family. I had never experienced any trauma in my life before this.

An RV driving by saw the accident and stopped. The concerned couple brought us kids into their RV to remove us from the scene and tried to comfort us. I kept feeling like this whole thing wasn't happening to us. It couldn't be our family that was in a horrific car accident.

I remember my dad coming into the RV, sobbing. Between his heaving sobs of anguish, he kept repeating how sorry he was. He didn't know how to tell Mom. As I listened to him, I just kept thinking to myself:

"I should have driven…"

This was such a difficult experience for me. It was a defining moment for me, and it helped give me perspective on the value of life. As the morning came and we had to deal with all the aftermath of this horrific accident, I had a thought come into my mind that changed everything.

Am I a victim or a survivor of this experience?

At that time, I knew I was both. I was a victim of a traumatic car accident, and I had also survived the accident. But how would I decide to identify myself? What would be the story I told others? For some reason, I didn't want to be a victim OR a survivor. I wanted to be something more. I didn't want the loss of my brother to be something that I feared talking about. I didn't want driving to be something I cowered away from. I didn't want our family to fear our future or our past.

In the weeks following the accident, I kept thinking about what a person who had risen from tragedy would do. I decided I could learn from the passing of my brother Danny the best way I knew how. I would conquer my fears and face the future that he would never be able to. This isn't to say that I didn't still have setbacks or struggles, but I consciously created a new focus on becoming a better human being. The death of my brother woke me up to an entirely new perspective on life. I had so many questions about my experience. I also had so many questions about how others handled their own experiences.

What leads people, who are in the same difficult circumstances, to see themselves as either a victim or survivor? What makes them strive to be more than just a survivor, face very tough circumstances, and rise above them? How can people take those same skills and use them in the face of their fears?

These are questions I have been asking myself since Danny's death. They are the questions that I ask myself after every tough challenge in my life. This is a difficult part of my life to share. I believe that if you and I were to sit down together and talk, you could share a trying time in your life, too—a time when you found yourself struggling, lost, mourning, etc. The reason I wanted to share this part of my life in this book is to show that we ALL have struggles. We all face adversity, heartache, pain, and suffering.

But it is what we do after the adversity that makes all the difference. It is taking the experience, learning from it, and discovering how it can help in all areas of our lives—including our businesses.

Circumstances are things that happen outside of ourselves and our control. The car accident was a circumstance. The weather is a circumstance. Other people's actions are also circumstances. These

THE GAME OF CONQUERING

can't be changed. What we **CAN** change is how we experience the circumstances that HAVE happened to us or are currently happening to us. Our thoughts and feelings lead us to the experiences that we will have. If we have thoughts of being a victim, we will most likely become a victim. So how do we know if we are showing up as a victim, survivor, or conqueror of our lives?

This book won't make anything easy, but it will make it easier. No one has ever accomplished anything worthwhile and said, "That was easier than I thought it was going to be." The test is part of the testimony. The struggle is part of the story. Neither the test nor the struggle mean much unless we learn from them and overcome them.

I believe there are three different types of mindsets that lead us in completely different directions in both our network marketing business and in our lives. Do you know the difference between a victim, survivor, and conqueror in network marketing? How can we change and rise to conquer the circumstances in our lives that we can't change? How can we finally transition into conquerors in network marketing? What are the steps needed to overcome the fears that are preventing us from doing what we know we need to do?

Victim, Survivor, and Conqueror—each one of these mindsets have a different way of viewing and interacting with the world and its circumstances. They each bring different thoughts and attitudes into our lives and, in turn, create different results. The next several chapters will dive into each one of these three mindsets, how to identify them, and how we can change them to create what we want.

VICTIM

SURVIVOR

CONQUEROR

"When you think everything is someone else's fault, you will suffer a lot. When you realize that everything springs only from yourself, you will learn both peace and joy."

-14th Dalai Lama

CHAPTER 2
VICTIM

Before I tell you more about victim mindset, I want to acknowledge something important. There is strength in identifying as a victim. Being a victim is NOT a weakness. It is part of the process we all need to go through. We have all had circumstances happen in our lives we were victims of. When I talk about **victim mindset**, I am not speaking to people who have gone through trauma and have done the work needed to heal from past trauma. I am also not speaking of people who are currently dealing with trauma.

Victim mindset and victim are very different. In the dictionary, **victim** is defined as "one that is injured, destroyed, or sacrificed under any of various conditions," or "one that is subjected to oppression, hardship, or mistreatment." **Victim mindset** is an acquired personality trait in which a person tends to recognize him or herself as a victim of the negative actions of others and will behave as if this were the case, even in the face or contradictory evidence.

People with victim mindsets live in the past. They are defined by the past. They blame past experiences rather than taking ownership of their part. The victim mindset has **Zero Accountability**. They cannot see how to create a way to get themselves out of their current thought patterns, because most of the time, they don't even see the thought pattern! They completely disregard their own agency and keep repeating their current circumstances. It rarely occurs to them to change either their mindset or the circumstances. They don't use their agency to choose something different. They use the victim card to play on the sympathies of others.

A thought that victims frequently have is, "Why me?" The victim mindset is selfish because everything is always about them. The victim mindset believes their difficult experience should never have happened. They find their thoughts consumed by this. Victims find the negative in their experiences. Victims are pessimists. Victims are blamers.

They often try to bring up their past experiences with others to get sympathy or attention. They may also lie about actual events to gain more sympathy. Someone with a victim mindset may even cut others out of their life if they don't buy into their victim story. Growth becomes stagnant when anyone gets stuck as the victim. The victim mindset is draining on the person who has it, as well as to those around them.

People with a victim mindset have a hard time seeing things differently, and they resist change to their story. Blame and excuses will be put on everyone or everything around them, and rarely will they take accountability. Those with the victim mindset see it as a benefit to not have to take responsibility for their own choices. They love the attention they get from their stories and feel that it makes them interesting and validated.

I spoke in nine different countries last year for several different network marketing companies. I can tell you that I had almost the exact same conversation with many different people in each of the nine countries in a variety of different companies. It goes something like this:

OTHER PERSON: "Rob, you need to know something about our area."

ME: "Let me guess. Your area doesn't like network marketing. The people in your area are closed-minded and think differently."

OTHER PERSON: "Wow! How did you know? You understand us!"

This conversation happens in every country I visit. This conversation happens in every city I visit in the U.S. Each city and country also provides a few additional reasons WHY it is "harder" to build in their particular area vs other areas.

KNOW THIS: Conquerors focus on and create their success story, while victims waste their time creating their alibis. A Conqueror always reacts to difficult circumstances to turn a negative into a positive.

A person with a victim mindset may also struggle with feelings of worth and value. They will see how their circumstances have made them less than others, and unworthy of being loved or accepted. In other words, they feel they don't deserve success and will act in ways to turn those feelings into truth.

A person with the victim mindset may feel damaged, hopeless, and struggle with feelings of shame. People with this type of mindset will try to hide their stories, and they will not seek help because of the shame they feel from their circumstances. Hiding will once again make growth stagnant and will keep this person in the victim mindset. Learn to stay in your low moments for less time and get into action as soon as possible. Everyone feels down at times, but people who learn to conquer understand how these low moments are just that—a moment. Embrace your struggles one day at a time.

Victims in network marketing blame everyone and everything else. They think the products are too expensive and will find anything wrong with them that they can. They blame shipping for being too expensive. They blame the compensation plan. They believe their leaders aren't helping them enough. Victims believe that many who were successful became so because of luck and refuse to believe otherwise.

I met someone after a speaking engagement who wanted to spend time telling me why the company, upline, and downline, were all responsible for their failure. As I listened, I could hear how everything OUTSIDE of this person was the reason why he hadn't found success. This person kept asking me, "What should I do? What can I do when the world, my upline, the company, isn't cheering on my success?" You know what I told this person? Stop trying to find outside validation. Go and make it happen." It may seem a bit harsh, but I knew this person was in a complete victim mindset.

Victims are ASKHOLES. An ASKHOLE is a person who constantly asks for advice and then does the opposite of what you suggested. You are probably laughing right now because it is true. Watch out for those askholes!

Too many network marketers have some degree of the victim mentality. Victims blame their area and their circle of influence. They are so self-consumed they can't see the forest from the trees. Even though someone in their company with less of a skillset and a harder situation is outperforming them, they refuse to believe they are the problem. Instead, they continue to focus on all the problems outside of themselves.

You may not actually have a victim mentality yourself, but sometimes you are dealing with someone in your life or business who does. Too many network marketers never achieve their dreams because they are stuck wasting their time trying to please the victims. By wasting your time with victims, you will never have enough time to spend with those who deserve your time. Trust me—I know. I am a recovering people pleaser and it has taken me years and years of practice to spend my time with the right people.

So, let's recap. Here is how you can determine if you or someone you know is in a victim state of mind.

VICTIM MINDSET

- Lives in the past and defines their future based on past experiences

- Blames their circumstances on others and takes no accountability

- Views their product, the company, their area, etc., as the problem with their business

- Uses victim card to get sympathy and attention from others

- Stagnant growth and resistant to change

- Can be an ASKHOLE

- Feelings of always suffering

- Hides experiences from others because of shame

"I'm a survivor. I'm gonna make it.

I will survive.

Keep on survivin'."

-Destiny's Child

CHAPTER 3

SURVIVOR

This statement may surprise YOU:

SURVIVORS AREN'T SUCCESSFUL IN NETWORK MARKETING.

Most events and webinars are filled with survivors. Let me give you some tough love. If you are a survivor in network marketing, you will not have success. (Ouch!)

I want to help you recruit more. I want to help you create more retention. I want to help you create more duplication. I can't do that unless I can be very direct with you. I am by no means saying that being a survivor is bad. It is actually a very positive and necessary step forward. I am just being clear that it isn't enough to just survive. There is more.

The GOAL is progress. Progress should always be celebrated. If you are a victim transitioning into a survivor, you should celebrate. If you are a survivor transitioning into a stronger survivor, that should

THE GAME OF CONQUERING

be celebrating, as well. Becoming a **survivor** is the first step in your process to success—but it can't be the end goal.

Some words that come to mind when I think about survivor mindset are **endurance, resilience,** and **struggle**.

Survivor mindset usually has an inner drive that keeps the person moving forward. They believe in family, faith, or something bigger than themselves. A person with a survivor mindset often cares more about those around them than themselves. But survivor mindsets struggle personally with feelings of worth and feeling weak. They may also feel unworthy of being a survivor of their circumstances. Someone with a survivor mindset will feel like they are barely hanging on.

Endurance feels like the norm for the survivor mindset. They always feel as if they need to be enduring and will constantly evaluate people or circumstances that may threaten their survival. This is a survival skill that humans have been programmed with since the beginning of time. It is what helps keep us alive in life's biggest emergencies. But often, because of this programmed response, the survivor will find themselves in fight-or-flight mode during regular daily life activities. Survivors put too much focus on NOT QUITTING rather than winning. The distinction is critical.

I will often hear these words from a survivor: "Rob, I am willing to do whatever it takes! I am super committed to this. I will never miss an event. I am at all the trainings. I am reading about personal development." This person is showing up and not quitting, but are they thriving? Are they winning?

A survivor is able to recognize their role in their experiences, which enables them to move beyond their circumstances. However, they doubt their own abilities to move forward any further, because they lack confidence in themselves. They compare themselves to others and struggle to keep up. They want people to see them as the "picture of perfection." They struggle to be vulnerable because it will destroy their perfection and define them as a victim. They keep their past hidden. They have let go of the past, but they still struggle to move on.

Survivors are often in leadership roles and have great problem-solving skills. They learn quickly how to adapt. They are also known for their positive attitudes. These are all great qualities to have, but they are also a weakness for the survivor mindset. Like I said before, the survivor mindset will feel they can never show weakness or talk about struggles. It's as if they were hiding some terrible secret. They will hide their insecurities and weaknesses behind their strong traits. They have a hard time asking for help and will go to great lengths to make sure people continue to see them as a survivor.

Sadly, someone who stays in survivor mindset for too long may slip into victim mindset. The mental pressure and strain of being "strong" and being in fight or flight mode will take its toll.

"I have gone to all the events," they will say. "I have read all the books. Why am I not successful?" They may feel there is no relief and will see themselves as a victim. They didn't progress past the survivor mindset and shift into a conqueror's mindset! They will always see their role as being a survivor and feel like there is no relief from the struggle.

My friend, Cindy, was in network marketing for twelve years and never made a ton of money. She came to every convention. She attended weekly trainings. She was very consistent with her personal development. She was told that if you just don't quit, you will eventually succeed. But after twelve years into network marketing— that wasn't the case. She still hadn't achieved any of her goals.

Cindy, like most network marketers, wasn't effective with her time. She was just surviving. She was doing the least amount possible in the income producing activities. In her mind. she was working hard because she was always thinking about network marketing. But her

actions didn't reflect her goals. Her actions didn't reflect her dreams—
yet she was hoping for the business to take off.

She was what I call FAKE-WORKING. Working in this business is
talking to new people about your business or products. Cindy was
creating a checklist of 22 important things to do. Things like personal
development, team training, and studying the compensation plan. All
good things. But none of them mean anything if you aren't doing the
MAIN THING.

She was avoiding reaching out to new people because of FEAR. In this
case, fear is an emotion about the future. Fear is about something that
hasn't happened yet. If we don't learn to acknowledge and understand
our fears and conquer them, we will always be SURVIVORS—at best.
We will NEVER accomplish our goals, dreams, and aspirations. We
will survive, but we won't thrive.

To determine where you are at with your own mindset, here are the
overall characteristics of a survivor:

SURVIVOR MINDSET

- Has the power to endure

- Committed to networking events and personal development

- Watches most of the team trainings but won't take enough action about what was learned.

- Focused on NOT QUITTING instead of winning

- Possesses an inner drive and feelings of something bigger than themselves

- Seen as strong but may feel weak or unworthy

- Can recognize their role and move beyond their circumstances

- Compares themselves to others

- Keeps past hidden from others

- Spends time fake-working in their network marketing business

- Mentally exhausted from staying in survivor mindset too long

- Will not be successful in network marketing

"If you do not conquer self, you will be conquered by self."

-Napoleon Hill

CHAPTER 4

CONQUEROR

To rise from survivor to conqueror, you've got to stop feeling sorry for yourself. You've got to take full responsibility, and you've got to stop making excuses. You've got to start taking action in the right places in your life and your network marketing business. Because I promise you, you can make excuses—OR you can make things happen. But you can't do both.

Conquerors get so sick and tired of just surviving in their network marketing business that something inside of them finally clicks! While survivors have enough of the vision that they don't quit, **Conquerors** have enough of the vision that they take MASSIVE ACTION in the Income Producing Activities.

As a side note, in *The Game of Networking*, I talk all about how to take deliberate action in IPAs. This includes talking to new people, receiving third party validation, adding to your lead list, nurturing relationships, and team trainings. For more training on my exact Income Producing Activities for network marketers, go to **www.sperrybonus.com.**

I have created this FREE resource to help you FOCUS and produce more results. You will want these printed out and have them somewhere you can see them daily. These Income Producing Activities come from a combination of my own personal experiences and those of many other top earners. If you need help moving into a conqueror mindset—start with your IPAs.

In addition to taking swift action, a conqueror mindset embraces the past and learns from it. They see life and everything in it as an opportunity for growth. They have the ability to embrace their experiences and show sympathy and understanding. They love themselves, and their past, because they can see the growth that has come from it. They show gratitude for all their experiences—especially the hard ones—because of the lessons they have learned while in them. And most importantly, they seek to inspire change in others, because of the change they have witnessed in themselves.

Those with the conqueror mindset are willing to be vulnerable with others, and they live with authenticity. In my first book, *The Game of Networking*, I talked about being an authentic person who isn't afraid to show some weaknesses. To be likeable, you don't need to be perfect. In fact, many will love you because of your imperfections. It is because of those imperfections that people will be able to relate better to you. A person with a conqueror mindset understands this and puts it into practice.

Conquerors have **complete accountability**. Someone with a conqueror's mindset will accept that their present is made up of a series of decisions that they have made in the past. They will also recognize that the future is made up of a series of decisions they can start making today. Those with a conqueror's mindset know that sharing failures and past experiences, and being vulnerable, will allow others and themselves to grow and have better relationships. They are confident and secure enough to share openly and honestly with others.

When adversity does happen, a conqueror faces it. They don't cower away or try to run from it. They realize that adversity sometimes comes as a result of their own choices, and sometimes from the choices of others. Either way, they face adversity, deal with it, and learn from it. They seek support from those around them, when necessary. They also recognize that adversity can teach them. No matter how hard the experience is, they understand that with the support of others and a conqueror's mindset, they will be able to get through the experience and learn from it.

Someone with a conqueror mindset is committed to their growth. They refuse to settle for "good enough." They also know this type of mindset takes effort and work. They have set aside and dedicated time to work on it. They don't let harsh or negative words from others deter them from their path. They want to be an example of what is possible.

Thoughts drive feelings and actions. Someone with a conqueror's mindset doesn't allow thoughts to drive feelings in a direction they don't want to go. When negative self-talk creeps in, they don't create drama around it. They acknowledge it and move on. They think thoughts ON PURPOSE. Conquerors use the past as a tool from which to learn. They see the future as a motivator—and their present is what they focus on.

Last year, I created two mastermind groups. One was created for those who haven't made six figures but are striving to do so. I call that one the *6 Figure Breakthrough*. In this mastermind, we give specific strategies to help generate both accountability and breakthrough. I also have 6/7 figure earner masterminds twice a year. This mastermind is unlike anything out there! I put on events for these masterminds around the world and there is something VERY unique and different about these people than any other event I speak at.

These groups are made up of people with a conqueror's mindset. Not all started out with this mindset, either! Despite having the conqueror mindset more than most, they still have those moments of doubt and struggle. It was eye-opening seeing so many top leaders be VULNERABLE in sharing their struggles. One of the biggest insights I had was when I noticed that each leader stays in the victim or survivor mindset for far less time than the average person. Each and every one of them has learned about the conqueror's mindset and they intentionally put it into practice. Not only do they put it into practice, but they do it more often AND quicker. The results they have created in their network marketing business and personal lives is evidence of the power of the conqueror's mindset.

My friend Tracy had been in network marketing for over 30 years with no success. In July 2017, she was homeless and living out of her car. She bought my book, *The Game of Networking*, and as she read it, something clicked for her.

The combination of her circumstance and a newfound vision from the book gave her the clarity she needed to go all out and take MASSIVE ACTION in the income producing activities. She was ready to switch out of just surviving to conquering mode in her life and her business. She didn't blame her circumstances. She didn't blame her area. Surviving was no longer enough. She DECIDED to become a conqueror.

She became the top earner in her company within several months. She gave everyone my book as a blueprint to success. She followed every Facebook Live I did and shared it with her teams. That's the super easy part! The biggest key is—she **stopped fake-working**. She stopped pretending to work like most do in network marketing and she FOCUSED. She shifted into a conqueror and started to follow the Conqueror's Formula—a formula I will give you in the next chapter. Tracy was ready to become a conqueror. Are you?

If your answer is yes, read on! To be a conqueror, you have to learn how to change your current mindset. In the next chapter, I will share exactly how to do that, as well as explain the Conqueror's Formula. This is my system that I share with all of my mastermind groups to help them stay on track to continue to create the success and lives they want. It has also helped people just like Tracy become the type of person they want to be. It doesn't matter if you are a 6- or 7-figure earner in my mastermind, or someone just starting out in network marketing. This formula will help you take your business to the next level and help you become a person who lives and succeeds with a conqueror's mindset.

This is the mindset you need if you want to find success in your business.

CONQUEROR MINDSET

- Takes full responsibility and doesn't make excuses

- Focuses on The Income Producing Activities

- Takes massive action

- Embraces past and learns from it

- Understands that circumstances are outside of their control

- Loves themselves and their past experiences

- Seeks to inspire and connect with others through sharing experiences

- Also seeks support from others and honestly talks about what they are facing

- Commits to growth and sets aside time to work on mindset

- Thinks thoughts on purpose to drive their feelings and actions towards the life they want to create

- Follows the Conqueror's Formula to create success in their network marketing business

"I've come to believe that all my past failure and frustration were actually laying the foundation for understandings that have created the new level of living I now enjoy."

-Tony Robbins

CHAPTER 5

CHANGE YOUR MINDSET

If you could only read one chapter in this book—read this! Now this is some tough love, but I believe that most of you reading this book are survivors. You are survivors, but you have that conquering spirit. I want to help you become the conqueror you have always wanted to be.

You are sick and tired of playing small and of making excuses. You are sick and tired of being broke. You are sick and tired of having no time or freedom. You are sick and tired of having dreams but no time to create real memories. You are exhausted because you aren't living your life. You are merely surviving, at best. God didn't send you to this earth to fail. Nor did He send you to this earth to play small. He didn't send you here just to be average. You have potential, but potential is talent unrealized.

It is time for you to realize your talent.

It is time for you to do what it takes.

It is time for you to stop making excuses and start finding reasons to win.

In order to do this, you will have to start training and retraining your brain to see the positive and seek the good. You will have to train your brain to take action.

Remember I told you that I would share with you the Conqueror's Formula? This formula is all about action. These are actionable items for you to put into place to help you change your mindset. Now, I'm not the best at math, so the formula doesn't look like a math formula that will help you solve for the square root of anything. This is a formula you can learn and use to track your progress in your network marketing business and life. You can also keep referring to it if you find yourself stuck on the way to becoming a conqueror.

The Conqueror's Formula is also how I teach my mastermind community to find the areas in their business that are creating value, and then I work with them in such a way as to produce 10x more success for them.

THE CONQUEROR'S FORMULA:

$$\frac{Vision + Environment + Discipline + Habits}{Success}$$

Now, I could write a completely separate book about this formula. But I wanted to make sure to hit on the most important points about this because it is a tool that is crucial in taking your mindset to the next level. I will briefly mention and explain each of these and why they are important. If you want more info about the Conqueror's Formula, please check **www.sperrybonus.com** to find my free Conqueror's Formula success guide.

Let's begin with vision. **Vision** is what you think and intentionally believe your network marketing business and life could be. Your vision is your purpose and dream. Your vision is the whole reason why you decide to do anything. I like to call it your future focus glasses. If you put on these glasses, what would you see? What would your business be producing? What does your workday look like? What are you wearing? Where do you live and what are you driving? What are you doing on a daily basis? Put those glasses on and take a look. What type of future do you see for yourself? Make your vision as detailed as possible.

Vision of the future helps us see the difference between where we are now and where we want to be. When we can see the difference, we can start putting together a vision map to know what steps we need to take to get into our future vision from the present.

As Stephen Covey says in his world-famous book, *The 7 Habits of Highly Effective People*: "Begin with the end in mind."

For example, take working out. You can't say I am going to go to the gym to work out because it is the right thing to do. You need to have a compelling reason to want to go. Examples are: "I have a big beach vacation coming up, and I want to lose weight," or "My doctor told me I need to work out or I could have a heart attack." What would be your compelling reason?

The vision is what will motivate you to get there. If we lack motivation, then we lack vision. Your VISION must be stronger than your mood swings, or you will never accomplish that vision. If my vision for working out at the gym is weak, as soon as I am tired or busy, I will find an excuse to avoid going. If my vision is strong to get in shape for a wedding, then I will find the inner motivation to work out.

Tony Robbins gives a great example on how we make all of our decisions: "Every decision is based on two emotions. Our association to pain and pleasure. It is simple. If there is more pain than pleasure, your decision for working out will be to not go."

If you have more of an association with pleasure—to get fit for your wedding and how good that will make you feel—then you will work out. You need to create a very clear vision with an emotional association stronger on the pleasure side, or you will fail.

Look, I get it. Reaching out to new people is the scariest and hardest thing to do in network marketing. My fears on a scale of 1 to 10 were about a 9 as far as reaching out to new people. But my goals, dreams, ambitions, and VISION were a 10. My goals beat out my fears. My dreams beat out my fears. My ambitions beat out my fears. My vision beat out my fears. And it wasn't because my fears weren't MASSIVE. It was simply because my VISION was big enough. Having a huge vision is the most important step to the Conqueror's Formula, but it is just the start.

Environment is what you are surrounding yourself with throughout your day. This is both your physical surroundings and mental surroundings. Oftentimes, our environment is something that we don't always notice. It is something we have grown accustomed to, so the impact never occurs to us. We take our environment for granted. Take a look at the room you are sitting in right now. How does it make you feel? Is it a space for creativity, learning, growth? You can't develop discipline in a bad environment.

What about what you bring into your environment through what you are watching, listening to, or reading? Who do you follow on social media? If someone bothers you constantly on social media, then why are you allowing them to influence you negatively on a daily basis?

Who are your friends? If someone isn't uplifting your life, then you need to re-evaluate your associations. The law of association is one of the most important influencing factors in your life. We typically become like our five closest friends in all aspects of life. If you hang out with five negative friends, you will become the sixth.

I can always tell where people are at in their journey by having them list the last ten things they consumed through these outlets. Is your consumption creating the type of environment needed to be a conqueror? There are so many areas to examine in your environment—the daily and weekly visits to places around your community, the foods you consume, and the physical movement you take your body through. Look at each of these areas and see if there is room for improvement within your environment.

Let's look at an extreme example. If you are an alcoholic, you can't have a massive vision of sobriety and have bottles of liquor all over the house at the same time. You can't be focused on getting in great shape but then have every single one of your favorite desserts, candies, and unhealthy foods in your kitchen. You can't expect success in network marketing if you surround yourself daily with negativity. I had to listen to over 100 books on personal development my first 18 months in network marketing. I had to surround myself daily with positivity to help me overcome my fears. Make sure to examine your own environment and make the necessary changes.

Now that you understand both vision and environment, let's give you a different take on discipline that you probably have never heard of.

Discipline isn't going to take away from what you want. It is going to give you everything you ever wanted. Discipline is habitually showing up and putting dedicated practice into certain areas of life.

If you haven't set aside dedicated time to work on your IPAs (income producing activities) with your network marketing business, do you have discipline? Too often I hear people say, "I didn't feel like it." People are waiting for the perfect day, with the perfect weather, in the perfect place, with the perfect outfit, so they can meet the perfect contact.

Discipline goes back to training yourself to show up. A saying that I heard growing up is, "I always do what I ought to do; whether I want to or not; NO DEBATE." This is a great example of showing up and doing the work, not based on how we feel at the time, but because we are dedicated to our discipline. Truthfully, the time will never be "perfect."

Discipline becomes so much easier when you have the right vision and environment. Easier doesn't mean easy. Success is never easy. When I started network marketing over eleven years ago, I created several daily disciplines to help set me up for success.

I set goals to read personal development every day, exercise every week, say prayers and read scriptures daily, have a date night with my wife Janei'a weekly, make time to do something with my kids on a regular basis, reach out via text or call every day to someone in my business, and lastly, I had a goal of making 100 phone calls—daily—that were related to my business. Yes, some of those goals may seem like they have nothing to do with network marketing—but they did to me.

My family and spiritual goals were part of my vision for network marketing success. I didn't want to work so hard on my business that I lost sight of what I was working for. Because I knew I was about to become obsessed.

It's over a decade later, and I want to give you a few updates. Last year, I did seven family vacations. I won't brag about cars or houses, but I will always brag about family vacations because that is what motivates me. I haven't missed one day reading personal development in over a decade. I have only missed one day of spiritual reading in the last decade. I haven't missed one day saying my prayers, and I haven't missed an entire week of working out in over a decade. Show me your disciplines and I will show you your future.

I get it—my goal of 100 calls a day became laughable as I transitioned into building my business online. But back when I set that goal, there was no social media focus. The principle is the same, but the social media platforms helped me reach more people quicker.

Why is discipline so hard in network marketing? Your parents, teachers, coaches, and bosses all told you what to do. Now you can do what you want, when you want. That may sound incredible—but it isn't easy. Too many network marketers focus on Tomorrowland. I will do that tomorrow. I will do that someday. You need to create the right daily disciplines to set yourself up for success. Someday is TODAY.

I don't want you to just think this book was helpful. I want you to CHANGE and progress. That's why I am going all out on additional FREE resources and sharing them throughout this book to help you implement what you learn. Go to **www.sperrybonus.com** to get my FREE training on a DMO (daily method of operation) for success in network marketing.

Habits are simply the consistent and repeated daily practices that will help us bring our vision to life. Everyone has habits. Many experts believe we make 35,000 decisions a day and 40 percent of those decisions are habits. Go through your day and write down what your habits are. Find the places in your life and your network marketing business and determine where your habits need a boost or a change.

What pieces of the map can you put into place with your habits to help your vision happen?

Create the right habits and you cannot fail. Create habits so strong that it isn't a question of if you will be successful—but when you will be successful. Again, show me your habits and I will show you your future.

This is it—that's the Conqueror's Formula. Vision + Environment + Discipline + Habits = Success. It really is that simple!

Now, our brain is naturally fearful—it's naturally negative. Your mind will play "worst case scenario" games and think of all the reasons why you can't succeed. You may look at the Conqueror's Formula and see flaws. You may think it is too simple or too hard. Your brain is always looking for things that threaten its way of living. It will force you to simply survive because you lack the courage to step outside of your comfort zone. It is crucial for your success to train your brain to work for you, rather than against you.

This is exactly what I had to do with my brother's death. In order to conquer my experience with Danny's death, I had to view it differently. It has now become the best thing that ever happened to me. That may sound crazy, but I am ten times the person I was because I walked through that experience. The circumstance of losing Danny cannot ever change, but my thoughts about it can.

That experience makes me appreciate every single day. It helps me appreciate every single person. And it helps me appreciate every single relationship. It helps me to overcome the natural tendencies and fears I have. YOU have the ability to change your own thoughts about your circumstances, and you can do it today. My experience with Danny's death gave me an opportunity to appreciate the NOW.

Changing your mindset is not easy! The Victim, Survivor, and Conqueror mindsets are experienced by everyone at different times in their lives. It is our responsibility to cycle through them and continue our progression. I learned from John Maxwell that everything worthwhile is harder than we think it is going to be

I understand this principle, having learned it early in life as I played tennis. I saw so many kids start, but when training picked up, and the time commitment became greater, they quit. It was too hard. Years later they would ask me how tennis was going. And when I told them what I was up to in the tennis world, they would say something like, "I wish I would have stuck with it." Now they could have picked it back up and started again, but the commitment was, once again, too hard.

When I first started in network marketing, I was an emotional rollercoaster. When someone great joined my business, I got way too high. I literally started envisioning myself traveling the world and retiring. The opposite happened, as well. When someone good quit my business, I became a Drama King. I didn't show it on the outside, but internally I would question network marketing. I was too high when things went well and too low when things went bad. We need to learn to fight our way toward progress. We need to learn to fight to do our very best and become the best version of ourselves. Another useful formula to remember: inaction = no change.

This fight begins in our minds. The inner struggle is so real. It literally changes how we deal with our daily lives. Our thoughts, our mindset— what we have on repeat in our heads—is critical to this process. What are you telling yourself? DECIDE ON PURPOSE what thoughts you will play in your head. I don't know about you, but sometimes if I leave my thoughts up to my brain, they can get pretty negative, pretty fast! Our thoughts are what tell us how to interpret the world around us. Fight with your mind to rationalize everything to help you succeed. Don't give into the victim mentality, blaming everyone and everything else. Anything that happens to YOU will only make you stronger and more resolved because you have a learner's mentality. You are a conqueror who looks to use every experience as a way to learn, grow, and become better.

Looking at your fears is a great way to understand how your mindset and thoughts are showing up in your life. Seeing your mindset deal with your fears is the work we will do together for the rest of this book. We will be looking at several different fears and how victim, survivor, and conqueror mindsets will take on these fears. I will also tell you about the one fear that rules them all. The one underlying fear I found that's at the root of all our fears in network marketing.

Dale Carnegie said, "If you want to conquer fear, don't just sit at home and think about it. Go out and get busy." Are you ready to get busy? As you read through this book, I want you to be taking notes about yourself.

WHERE DO YOU SEE THE THREE DIFFERENT MINDSETS IN YOUR OWN LIFE?

_____

_____

_____

_____

_____

CAN YOU IDENTIFY YOUR FEARS?

_____

_____

_____

_____

MINDSET CHANGE

- You can retrain your brain to work for you—anytime a negative thought comes to your mind, write down 3 solutions

- Our minds are naturally fearful and need to be retrained

- Mindset changes take intentional work

- You can't always change circumstances

- You CAN change your own thoughts about circumstances

- You can create YOUR story

- Become the conqueror and change the world

- Conqueror's Formula: Vision + Environment + Discipline + Habits = Success

OUR GREATEST FEARS:

FAILURE, INADEQUACY, MISSING OUT, THE UNKNOWN, BEING JUDGED

The brain is programed to keep us safe and avoid perceived dangers. Fear can come from real or imagined danger. Fear can be of something physical or emotional. It is one of the hardwired parts of our brains that has been passed down from generations to help keep us safe and alive. It is one of the most primal programs we have.

Having fears does not make you broken. Everyone has fears. Whether you are the CEO of a major organization or a soccer mom with five kids. Our brains are naturally fearful. Fear is a part of everyday life. Our success in life comes from recognizing our fears and learning how to deal with them with a conqueror's mindset. The conqueror's mindset doesn't ignore the fear. The conqueror's mindset doesn't live in fear. The conqueror's mindset identifies the fear and finds ways to use the fear to move forward with courage.

Fear is the #1 reason why people failing in networking marketing. It is also the #1 reason most people don't even start a network marketing business. They are afraid. They want their life to be different, but they aren't willing to do anything different to make it change.

MY FEARS ALMOST BEAT MY DREAMS

In 2008, I had been the wannabe entrepreneur for years. I was always coming up with ideas, but never pursuing them for fear of failure. I know it sounds silly, but my FEAR of FAILURE was so great that I was full of ideas and empty on ACTION.

In 2008, when I was approached about network marketing, I was TERRIFIED.

I was fearful of what others would think.

I feared failure.

I had this constant inner battle with my dreams vs my fears.

I knew my fears were ridiculous, but I couldn't seem to overcome them. I hated myself for letting such absurd fears control me.

My fears almost beat my dreams.

My first two days in network marketing, I called only one person. I couldn't muster the courage to call anyone else! Then I wrote this in my phone and EVERYTHING CHANGED:

"I have never tried to go all out and do something completely different because I am always scared of failing. I will go forward no matter what. When I get rejected, I will just become more determined. This is my break and opportunity. I deserve this right now!"

I literally had to read that statement over and over again. That statement empowered me to push through my fears. That statement was read, on some days, twenty times—because I was so fearful and felt paralyzed. I was way too prideful to admit my fears. Instead, I kept all of my greatest fears to myself.

If you are struggling right now, please don't let your fears beat your dreams. We all struggle at different points in our lives. But giving up on one's dreams has NEVER SOLVED ANYONE'S PROBLEMS. It may seem easier to quit on your dreams, but the easy road always ends up being the harder road! There are no shortcuts to success

✗ BEAT YOUR FEARS WITH DREAMS BY FOCUSING ON WHAT YOU WANT, RATHER THAN WHAT YOU DON'T WANT.

We get so caught up in our fears. It happens to the best of us. Our brains are wired to find danger around us and to avoid it. We get lost in the thoughts of fear. We let those fears run the show and don't take the necessary steps to get over them. As I said before, our brains literally use fear to keep us safe. But we have to remember that the majority of the fears are imagined! We think they are true. The fact is, even when we feel fear, it doesn't mean there is actual danger.

Look, everything worthwhile is almost always a little scary. But what's even scarier is being average. You weren't sent to this earth to be average!

"Growth comes from outside your comfort zone."

You were meant for GREATNESS.

We each have different fears that our brains focus on. What one person sees as fearful, another person would not even bat an eye at. Fear is based in the future. Regret is based on the past. Fear is the brain trying to keep us safe by presenting us with a host of different things that could happen. Let me repeat that. <u>Fear is an emotion focused on the future.</u> <u>Fear is focusing on events that have not happened and are unlikely to happen.</u>

I have been in this industry for a long time, and I have seen or heard every fear there is with network marketing. People are afraid of what others will think of them. They are afraid they don't know enough about the product. They are afraid the company is a fraud. They are afraid they will pass out or have a panic attack presenting in front of others. I really have heard it all!

Back in 2019, I did a poll in *The Game of Networking* Facebook group. I asked: "What is the hardest part of network marketing?" The answer shocked me. The hardest part for the majority of people in the group was the fear of what others think. People then commented and told me other hard parts of the industry. Time and time again, I saw the word "fear" in the comments.

As I listened to the fears associated with this business, I found there are five fears that all the fears can be categorized into. These fears seem to be present in people before they even start, once they start the work, as they grow their network marketing business, and sometimes even after they have success.

In these next chapters, we are going to discuss the top fears in network marketing, and how the three different mindsets react to those fears. I will give you specific tools to help you crush the fear and confidently step into the conqueror mindset. The steps to become a conqueror WILL require you to walk outside of your comfort zone and do things you would not normally do. But growth happens when we step outside our comfort zone and face our fears in a new and courageous way. Go face your fears and become the person you were meant to become.

You can build your network marketing business from fear or faith, but you can't do both. You have to decide which one you are going to feed.

Find your courage—and dig in. We've got work to do.

"There is only one thing that makes a dream impossible to achieve: the fear of failure."

-Paulo Coelho

CHAPTER 6

FAILURE

Stephen King is one of the bestselling authors of all time. He has hundreds of books published and has a net worth of 400 million dollars. His first book, *Carrie*, was rejected 30 times.

Failure was something he experienced over and over again. But eventually, the fear of failure for a lifetime got the best of him. He gave up submitting the book to publishers and threw the book away in the trash.

His wife fortunately got it out of the garbage and encouraged him to try again. We all know what happened after that. *Carrie* is known for being the epic horror novel that was later turned into a movie.

Stephen King is such a great example of overcoming a fear of failure to become hugely successful.

One of the most common fears I have experienced throughout my life, and the first fear I want to tackle, is the fear of failure. Everyone experiences the fear of failure in their life on a recurring basis.

We are afraid to fail in our network marketing business because it may reflect something negative about us, the company, or the product. One of my clients in *The Game of Networking* Facebook group said, "I am afraid to fail, because it will mean that all the naysayers were right about me, and about network marketing."

Another person said, "Each 'yes' or 'no' I get in my network marketing business is directly tied to my self-worth and how I view my own success in life." To this person, the fear of failing means their innate value is on the line. When we tie our own worth into our success or failure, we will always be afraid of failing. The fear of failure holds many people back from even showing up and trying.

When we fear failure, we will automatically find ways to avoid it. We don't see the learning opportunities and experiences that are available from all failure or success. At times, this fear will keep us tethered to past mistakes and regrets. It will keep us locked away from the world to not only avoid it, but the people in it. It will keep us from making decisions and moving forward. Understand the process of failure and it will provide you with more vision on what success really looks like. Failure is the sweat of success. You can't build your success muscles without working hard and sweating. You can't experience success without failure.

THE VICTIM MINDSET

When I was sixteen years old, the leader of my church came to my house and asked me if I would be willing to speak in church in front of our congregation of 300 people. He told me my message was something others needed to hear, and that I could have a positive impact on other people my age.

I politely told him I was sorry, but I wasn't willing to speak in church.

I knew what the right thing to do was, but my fear of failing in front of 300 people was so great that I remained selfishly consumed in my own insecurities. I was terrified of being bad. I was terrified of making a huge mistake and having everyone laugh at me. I was terrified of fumbling over my own words. I wasn't willing to put myself out there and risk messing up.

It has been said that FEAR stands for Fantasized Experiences Appearing Real. It has also been said that 90% or more of our fears never really happen. What was I so scared of? Why was my perception of messing up deemed a failure in my mind?

With the fear of failure, or any other fears, the victim's mindset is very negative. The victim believes that because of their circumstances, and their past, they will never be successful. They tell themselves, "I am going to fail anyway, so why even try?"

I share the fact that I wasn't willing to speak in church because too many people always hear the highlights of one's success. They think one has the perfect style or personality for what they are doing. Most people don't know that, although I speak all over the world now, there was a time when I not only was a little fearful of speaking—but it was one of my biggest fears.

Speaking wasn't my only fear. I remember early on in my college years, I was still struggling with math like I had throughout all of my school-age years. But the pressure was on now because I had to keep my grades up to be eligible to play tennis on the college team.

I felt immense pressure to pass a math class. I was so afraid of not being able to get a good grade based on my own knowledge. If I didn't pass, it would have resulted in me losing out on the opportunity to play tennis. Tennis was life. I couldn't imagine not being able to play tennis for my college. The pain of not having that in my life made me feel desperate. So, I made one of the biggest mistakes in my life.

I cheated.

At the time I thought, "If I don't get caught, the reward is worth the risk."

I played the victim. Instead of putting in the effort, I took a shortcut and I justified my actions, because the pain of the consequence felt too great.

This is a challenge to write. Millions (I like to think big) of people may read this, but the challenge is in the fact that my kids read all my books, too. I have guilt about cheating and writing about it at this moment brings forth the shame of my actions again. But it is important for me to acknowledge that we all make mistakes. Mistakes can be learning opportunities, and a chance for all of us to rise.

We can do better than taking the shortcut.

Oftentimes, I find that the shortcut takes us so much longer than we anticipate. We could learn what we need for the first time, and not have to make up the distance later. Shortcuts are NEVER the way. Figure out the right way the first time and do what you need to do.

In order to do this, you have to have perspective. We are in a society of instant gratification. Instant gratification usually makes us happy or solves problems short term. It puts off the bigger picture—and sometimes impedes it. If we can learn to delay gratification, put in the work, and stick with the path, we can reap long-term rewards and find true success.

One of my trusted mentors, Lon, taught me that true wealth is ability.

Victims allow fear to stop them from moving forward before they even take the first step. It's a vicious cycle that is continually perpetuated by their own belief. They fear failure, so they never try, and because they never try, they never succeed.

We all have insecurities, but most of us are too scared to admit them. I still have insecurities that I am overcoming. Growing up I had many more, which I have now overcome, but it is still a process. As I reflect back on the things that caused me anxiety, I realize that I have felt a lot of embarrassment in the past from things that I feared I would fail at. My wife hasn't even heard some of these things, but I thought I would share a bit about what I fear failing at. Here goes...

I have never dived into any water. Yes—I am talking about diving. Nope—no diving into a pool, lake, or ocean.

Crazy, huh?!

Embarrassing, huh?!

Somewhere a family member is reading this trying to think of a time I would have dove into the pool, but they can't because it never happened. They are probably both laughing and confused. Yes, I know it's confusing to think someone can now speak in front of thousands of people but hasn't ever taken a dive.

I'll give you another embarrassing fact about me due to my own fears. Up until two years ago at a Daddy-Daughter dance, I had never fast-danced once in my entire life. Not once! I was so scared of what others thought of me. I was so scared of not being great that I never even tried.

The crazy thing is, I went to every single high school dance! Many of you have been to junior high dances. There wasn't one kid back then, at my junior high dances, that had amazing dance skills. If I would have just jumped in and had fun with my friends, I wouldn't have had this particular fear of failure.

The longer I didn't dance, the bigger the fear of failure became. I was too scared to start, when I should've just joined in with everyone else. The boys that danced in junior high became boys that danced in high school, in college, and at concerts. I could've been one of those boys. That's a HUGE insight.

THE LONGER WE AVOID OUR FEARS THE MORE WE FEED THEM AND THE BIGGER DEAL THEY BECOME.

When all the other dads started dancing with their daughters at this dance, I felt completely sick to my stomach. I wanted to show up for my daughter, but I was terrified STILL of failing. Luckily my WANT outweighed my fear of dancing. It wasn't pretty. My dancing. Remember the dancing scene from the movie Hitch with Will Smith? Now go five notches below that!

I am still not the crazy person that tries everything. I may be considered boring to other people, but the point is that I am progressing. I am overcoming some of my natural tendencies. I am becoming self-aware of the difference between a victim, survivor, and conqueror. And I am choosing to no longer be the victim.

I want to stop for a moment and ask you these questions: What are you failing at because you are too scared to try? What would you try if you knew you could not fail?

One of my greatest fears when I began the network marketing profession was the fear of failure. I didn't want to be that person who tried and failed. Failure to me, at that time, was not making money on a monthly basis. Remember when I said that my first two days into network marketing, I called only one person? I was creating excuses in my head.

After those two days Lon, my mentor, called me. He was pretty brash, to say the least, and it was exactly what I needed. He asked how many new contacts I had made the last two days, and who was interested in at least taking a look. I flat out lied and told him I had a ton interested. I was just trying to buy time.

Lon then very directly told me the following: "Rob, you get me on the phone with someone right now, or I will never work with you again. It is now or never. If you don't get me on the phone with someone interested, then we are still friends. But if you want to make this business happen, you need to understand that urgency is synonymous with wealth. I don't want to hear about later. I don't want to hear about tomorrow."

Wow! He kicked me in the butt. Now understand, Lon had made millions of dollars and was a good friend. I had never seen that type of intensity from him, but he knew that if he waited for two more days, my fear of failure would have grown. It would have been huge enough that I would have quit. That one conversation saved me from quitting.

Yes, I understand that for many of you, that type of conversation would have made you quit. There is no perfect conversation. The main point is I had massive fears and needed someone to kick me in the butt. I will give you a good kick in the butt several times in this book to help YOU become aware of where you are and how to progress to the next level.

As I have grown older, my family has pointed out that I am actually more willing than ever to try new things. Most people are the opposite. But as I discovered and studied the topic of being a victim, survivor, or conqueror, I knew that I needed to do more. I knew I needed to be more.

I have also discovered that there can be a middle ground. Learning doesn't have to be all or nothing. Trying is just as valuable as succeeding. When we try our best to do new things, even if we don't do them well, there is success to be had, in having the courage to try. Just because we're not good at something doesn't mean we shouldn't do it. Trying new things leads to learning new lessons. It doesn't matter if you win or lose, it's how you play the game—or the lessons you learn from the game—that make the most difference.

THE SURVIVOR MINDSET

I have had many experiences with this in my life, but the one that sticks out to me the most is in my schooling. And it wasn't someone else's voice in my head, it was my own.

Not only was I extremely short and skinny growing up, but I was held back from the first grade. My parents tried to spin it to me as a positive thing because I could be the oldest in my grade. But I knew deep down that I hadn't done very well at school.

My school life was a struggle. I was never a great student, and school never came naturally to me. I told myself I was not great at school, and I never gave it my full effort. I focused instead on just getting by. I lacked the faith in my abilities to do anything better.

My narrative was easier than showing up and doing the work. I could have given it more effort and maybe found success. But instead, I told myself that I didn't have to spend time on being a better student. I focused on playing tennis and bet that my abilities on the court would get me into college. My story was that I wasn't a good student. I would survive school, but never succeed. How often do we sabotage ourselves before we start by only partly showing up? How would things be different if we always gave our very best?

As a survivor, I didn't let my circumstances get me down, but I didn't allow them to lift me up and grow from them either. I just simply survived.

Survivors do not allow themselves to be defined by their past. They choose to see beyond their circumstances and strive to overcome any past or present trauma. They have a desire to move forward and begin taking steps in the right direction. Survivors are willing to try, but they lack belief in themselves. They question the steps they are taking. This doubt leads to more frustration, they cannot move forward, and despite the positive steps that have been made, they still are unable to succeed and conquer.

I am sure all of us have experienced the fear of failure as a survivor. Does this sound familiar? You have a great idea you know will make a difference in your life and in the lives of many others. You start taking steps to make it happen. You may even achieve moderate success with it.

Because of sheer grit and determination to fight, survivors are able to be somewhat successful even if the fear of failure follows them. They put their emotions in an invisible box, place it on their invisible shelf, and do their very best to forget that it even exists. When events in their life trigger these ignored emotions and they start to surface, survivors will stuff them back down again. They have an undoubted determination and belief that they are strong enough to stop themselves from feeling.

But then, after your first initial steps with your great idea, you start getting kick-back from those around you. Your friends may say you are making a huge mistake and that you don't have the skills to make it happen. Someone you consider a professional tells you that you will never make it in the field, and that you might as well give up—so you do. Or, rather than giving up, you just hang around.

As I mentioned before, most people who are at big events in network marketing are survivors. They are doing the least amount possible to stick around. They don't quit but they don't take the necessary action to succeed. Deep down, they know they are just doing the busy work. The fake work! They are watching every training. They are studying all the ingredients to the new products. They are at every event… but they aren't reaching out to many new people! They are fake-working. They are merely surviving! Some of you are listening too much to those negative voices—including your own.

You listen to all those negative voices, telling you who you are and what you should become—and you believe them.

It is only when we take our thoughts about the circumstances and allow them to move us forward that we can move from the mindset of a survivor to a conqueror. The shift to conqueror comes by way of the stories we tell ourselves, and what we choose to believe. In effect, we are not our circumstances. We are what we think we are.

Even with the narrative I told myself about being bad in school, I did not let it define me. My whole life, I could have made excuses stemming from that narrative. I could have made so many excuses for not being smart and have it stifle my ambitions, but I didn't. And that is what led me to move from a survivor to a conqueror.

CONQUEROR MINDSET

Conquerors have a unique way of viewing failure: They see failure as a valuable tool for growth. And they have an incredible ability to turn their weaknesses into strengths.

When my brother died in that car crash, I had three options. I could have lived as a victim, revisiting that moment over and over again, blaming myself for his death because I didn't drive when my father asked me to. And to be honest, I did make that choice, and stayed in that place of feeling I failed my dad and my family, for a time. But my ability to be a fully functioning member of society would have greatly diminished had I chosen to stay there. I would not be the man I am today had this been my choice.

My second choice could have been to stuff down the pain and the emotions and denied their existence. I could have lashed out at my father for not pulling over sooner and blamed him for my pain. I could have spent my whole life lashing out at the world for the injustice that came from my brother's tragic death. But that choice would have led me to alienate my family and friends. Had I made this choice, I would not have the supportive community I now embrace.

My third choice was to feel the pain, to mourn the loss of my brother while showing gratitude for the time he was alive. Because of his death, I choose to hug those I love more and judge others less. I choose to use his death as a tremendous opportunity for growth to help me evaluate who I am and who I want to be in this life.

I treasure my time with my brother and hold those memories close. And when I look back on that accident, the only emotions I feel are gratitude and love for family and for the value of life. Because I allowed myself to feel the pain—to experience the feelings of failure in the moment—these feelings were eventually replaced. They were replaced with the joy of family and the hope that I would one day see my brother again. I truly believe there is a life after death—and that my brother is there waiting for me.

As hard as it is to imagine, I believe the experience with my brother's death was the greatest experience of my life. It helped give me DAILY perspective. It helped me appreciate life. As strange as it may sound, death can give life even more purpose.

There isn't a day that goes by where I don't think about the brevity of life and the abruptness of death. I constantly think about it. Because I value life and I am keenly aware of how short it truly is, I think about my kids or my wife dying, on a daily basis. I know that may sound unusual for some of you reading this, but for me, it helps me live each day better. For me, it provides life with more meaning.

I want to tell you something that not everyone gets. Choosing to embrace the conqueror's mindset isn't easy. It is always a choice, and sometimes it is a hard one to make. Conquerors realize that if they don't allow themselves to experience failure, they will also miss out on the joy of success. They open their hearts and embrace all the emotions of life, even the painful emotions that come from failing. Conquerors let those feelings pass through them, learn from them, and then they let them go. They don't hold onto things that are damaging to their soul.

This does not mean that conquerors don't have bad days and difficult circumstances. We all do, regardless of our mindset. But conquerors realize that life is a series of ups and downs and it is important to take in all of it to learn valuable lessons. But they only hold onto those things that really matter—and let go of all the rest. They are not weighed down by regrets because they understand that in life, we learn as we go. Success is derived from experience, and experience is a result of making mistakes and learning from them. The past can't be changed, but it can be the best possible teacher.

Conquerors grasp that in order to overcome difficult circumstances, they have to see them from a different perspective. They remember their past, but they choose to remember from a place of learning rather than a place of victimhood. They strive to see the good that came from their difficult circumstances instead of getting caught up in the details of how they were wronged.

Conquerors are still honest about how they feel, even if what they feel isn't always positive. But they work through their emotions and feelings with the hope and honest belief that they are not always going to feel the way they do in that moment and that the future will be better. They don't forget their hardships, but they don't keep them in a place of sadness and regret—they see them as a tool for learning and growth. By viewing difficulties with a conqueror mindset, these experiences don't hold negative emotions. Instead, conquerors carry hope and gratitude for how far they have come.

Conquerors recognize that overcoming hardships requires a positive change in both thoughts and actions—as it is our thoughts and actions that keep us in places of sadness and pain. It is freeing to learn that we do not have to live with the pains of life. We can feel the pain, show gratitude for it, and allow it to move us forward with new eyes to see and a greater understanding of life and our place in it. Conquerors look at setbacks as set-ups for an even bigger comeback. All trials strengthen them.

So many of my trials have strengthened me. For example, I failed math. That shouldn't come as a surprise to you from what I have already told you. I had the hardest time focusing in school and told everyone I had ADHD.

School was like a totally different language to me, and I never did well in any subject. I even had a tutor personally help me with math and I still barely received a passing grade. I easily could have branded myself as dumb. But instead, I branded myself as smart—but not school smart.

My parents helped me understand that school was for discipline, but it had no real measure on how smart I was or was not. They were the best parents for building up my self-esteem. Huge credit goes to them for making me feel very smart in other areas of my life!

This experience became such a positive motivating factor in my life.

I decided I was going to find a positive spin on my negative report card. So, I researched the grades and schooling of the top money-makers in the world. What I found was that many millionaires weren't the best in school either.

This was encouraging to me and made me feel that I was in good company. I changed the narrative. Yes—I still kept the narrative that I was a bad student, but, being a bad student was actually a good thing, after all. It just meant I had a different skill set than the good students. My mind simply flipped a switch.

Being able to put a positive spin on your negative circumstances is the mindset of a conqueror. Conquerors believe in themselves and find other ways to succeed when met with obstacles or hardship.

I was able to be a conqueror in my own life through researching and writing a new narrative of how being a bad student was actually a good thing.

I created a theory of why millionaires have bad grades, with the research and facts to back it up. For me, I needed that research to believe the new narrative. I needed truth.

The Internet is filled with thoughts and stories of courageous people who have overcome exactly what you are struggling with. Find those people and use their stories to help you rewrite your own narrative. Find the facts that back up the story you want to tell, and use them to help tell your story. Find your truth and learn to believe in you.

The theory I developed allowed me to change my perspective on my circumstances and propelled me forward in a big way. It all began with a quote.

Mark Twain said, "Don't let schooling interfere with your education." And I absolutely believe that is true. It's the perfect quote for a kid who struggles with his schooling.

In the book *The Millionaire Mind*, Dr. Thomas J. Stanley conducted an extensive survey of over 1,000 millionaires in the United States. He approximated that the average collegiate GPA for a self-made millionaire is 2.76. People with the highest level of satisfaction are more likely to drop out of school, according to research from psychologist Edward Diener. They understand that success at school is only one skill set and they can use and grow other skills and be very successful.

The New York Times columnist, David Brooks, jokes, "You know all those morons who sat in the back of the classrooms goofing off? In a few years you're going to have a new name for them—Boss."

Reading those statistics and quotes was exciting to me. They inspired me and enabled me to believe in myself.

My theory (and it is just that—a theory) is those who don't get good grades are forced to be creative and network better. They don't have school as a resource. School is actually a liability, and the students are forced to innovate.

This theory only works for those who are ambitious. Obviously, if you aren't ambitious, and you don't do well at school, that is a recipe for disaster. But I have always been ambitious and could never quite figure out why school was such a struggle.

I think it's important to clarify here that I am not suggesting you avoid school. I am only suggesting that this could be why my GPA—and the average millionaire's GPA—was so low! I honestly believe it is because our minds work differently. We struggle with school—memorizing facts and concepts. We learn things differently, and in ways that aren't taught in a classroom.

I'm going to go a little deeper with you here. Most millionaires and successful people can be defined as innovative. Doesn't that word sound smart? I am changing the narrative. Words are powerful—especially when you are changing the narrative for success.

Innovative doesn't necessarily mean they are creative. Even if we break this down to root words, creativity is the creation of new ideas. Innovative is taking the initiative to take new ideas and turn them into reality. There are many creative people out in the world, but the successful ones are innovative enough to take their wild dreams and make them happen.

Because I did not do well in school, and had a low GPA, I couldn't rely on school as a resource for future employment and success. I had to become more innovative in finding ways to contribute to society and achieve success. And because of that innovation, I found the success I was seeking.

I would make an addition to the quote earlier by Mark Twain that reads, "Don't let schooling interfere with your education." Instead, I would say, "Don't let schooling interfere with your creativity to network for more." There can be value found in everyone, even a kid without school smarts.

With my new narrative, I found truth that allowed me to see myself in a different light. My weakness in school became one of my greatest strengths. It demonstrated that there is a place in the world for all people, regardless of their school smarts. It showed there was a place in this world for me and allowed me to believe in myself and to take action on my ambitions.

In network marketing, I even turned my label as an introvert into a positive. Dave Blanchard, who is the current CEO of the OG Mandino organization, has done well over 80,000 assessments on network marketers. He found that over 70% of network marketers consider themselves introverts. We all have a little bit of introversion and extroversion in us, and much of it depends on the situation.

Use everything to your advantage. I told myself that being an introvert, I was less intimidating. I also felt many would say to themselves, "If Rob can do this business, so can I." As an introvert, I am great at listening. I value strong connections. I literally use everything that has been perceived as a weakness and potential failure and flip the script.

Your narrative needs to demonstrate to you your own value. So, when all those naysayers tell you that you can't, you will know without a doubt that you can.

Through the conqueror mindset, you have to see your so-called "failures" from a different perspective. You have to take your weaknesses and turn them into strengths. That is where the growth comes from. And that is how you will find success.

HOW TO CONQUER FEAR OF FAILURE

Your story is not just what happens to you. Your story is your perception of what happens to you. Each experience can be told in many different ways. Two people can view the exact same experience completely different because of the story they tell themselves. You have the opportunity to look for the lesson and the positive in each experience.

You get to create your story. You get to decide what people hear when you share your story. You get to decide. How incredibly powerful is that? You can go from victim to survivor, and from survivor to conqueror, just by the story you tell yourself. You can change the world with your story. This is worth repeating. YOU CAN CHANGE THE WORLD WITH YOUR STORY. But—it all begins with the story you are telling yourself. What story do you tell yourself when you fail?

Success doesn't happen while we're sitting around. It happens when we are actively conquering those fears that keep us from moving forward. The cure for fear is action. As we conquer one fear at a time, we will find the power within ourselves to transform our lives in miraculous ways.

Each fear has its own set of problems and solutions. I have learned that as I devote time and energy to focusing on solutions, I am able to crush every fear that comes my way. I have also learned from my own experiences that conquering fear can be hard. But it can be achieved if we approach it with a plan and have the determination to implement that plan.

At the end of every chapter, I have outlined ways for you to face that chapter's fear and conquer it. It is my hope that you apply these principles to conquering and overcoming those fears that are keeping you stuck in life. I believe if you work at it, you have the ability to stand face-to-face with any fear that comes your way and prevail as a conqueror.

To get you started, if you struggle with the fear of failure, here are five ideas for you to apply to your life to help you conquer that fear.

- **SET ATTAINABLE GOALS.** Goals keep us focused. Goals help us measure success. I love dreaming big and setting high, lofty goals. But it is also vital to set and measure some of those goals on your personal efforts rather than just results. I understand that at times results are a measurement of our success. However, you must measure much of your success on your effort. Set goals that are based on your own personal effort. Set goals that are realistically attainable and measurable, and work towards them. Every time you reach a goal, reward yourself, and record it in a journal or somewhere you can track it so you can look back at all those things you have been successful at.

- **CHANGE YOUR STORY.** If you have always told yourself you are a failure, then most likely you will always be one. If you want to feel successful, focus on your successes and retain the mindset of a winner. Just like I did when I struggled in math, put a positive spin on your negative situation. Changing your story from negative to positive is a vital key to overcoming the fear of failure. Never say the words "I am" followed by a negative. Don't brand yourself in a negative way. Words are very powerful. Use them to your advantage.

- **STUDY YOUR WEAKNESSES.** I started out in life having a fear of speaking in front of others. Public speaking is now one of my strengths, and I get paid a lot to do it. I put a great deal of energy into researching and learning the skills needed to turn my weakness into a strength—and then I practiced. If you research your weakness and practice increasing your skills in that area, you are bound to turn your weaknesses into strengths, too. Read fifteen minutes a day on the weakness you are focusing on. Don't just read—implement. Take the things you learn and find ways to have small victories. Find ways to get out of your comfort zone. Those small victories will add up to tremendous changes.

- **SEE THE GOOD.** Be careful what you seek because you will find it. When you are in the midst of what you would consider a failure, write down three positive things that have come from it. Alter the way you see the situation. Instead of seeing it as a failure, write down what you learned from it and how it has helped you grow

- **STEP AWAY FROM THE NEED FOR PERFECTION.** This life is full of imperfect people. Mistakes are a part of everyday life and everyone, without exception, makes them. Instead of buying into the "perfect" lie, remind yourself often that no one is perfect. Create a motto such as, "Do your very best and forget the rest." When you feel pressured to be perfect, repeat your motto and remember, instead, that as long as you are doing your best, you are doing enough. Perfection is not required. In fact, the quest for perfection will only add stress and slow down your efforts to becoming a conqueror. The goal is PROGRESS not PERFECTION.

Many people believe that if they are not perfect, they are failing, but perfection is a myth we hold as a truth. At the same time, failure is a natural part of life and the learning process—yet we have defined it as something negative and undesirable. When we choose to change our perspective and see failure as an inevitable part of the human condition and embrace it as an opportunity for learning and growth, we no longer fear it. Becoming a conqueror is more than just overcoming your fears. It is changing your entire perspective and embracing those fears as good friends and teachers. When you can do this, your life will never be the same—and nothing will stop you from achieving your goals.

"Do your very best and forget the rest"

-You

"Our deepest fear is not that we are inadequate. Our deepest fear is that we are powerful beyond measure."

-Marianne Williamson

CHAPTER 7

INADEQUACY

I f you don't know by now, my wife and I are HUGE moviegoers. Date nights usually consist of dinner and a movie, and we are both positive we would be widely successful movie critics!

The name Tom Hanks is a household name across the planet. His career in the film industry started when I was a kid just getting into watching movies. My favorite Tom Hanks movie of all time is Forrest Gump. If you haven't seen it, go watch it!

It surprised me when I read an interview he gave after a 2016 role he had. Tom played an American businessman who had a lot of self-doubt. In the interview, Tom said, "No matter what we've done, there comes a point where you think, 'How did I get here? When are they going to discover that I am a fraud, and take everything away from me?'"

This blew me away when I read it. A hugely successful actor, who has been in the industry for decades, still battles with a fear of inadequacy.

We've all had those moments where we didn't believe we were enough for the task at hand. We don't have the skills, or we are just plain not good enough.

This fear has been a major factor in the lives of so many who have stopped moving forward and are living a life of mediocrity. It's not because of their fear of what others may say, but because of what they are saying to themselves. What we are saying to ourselves is so important. I see so many people who don't intentionally talk to themselves, and sadly, most human brains are set to the negative dial.

So many times, we become a stumbling block in our own progression because we can't be kind to ourselves. Instead, we end up tearing ourselves down so much that we are paralyzed from moving forward. We incessantly analyze our abilities and put all our focus on our inadequacies that this analysis turns into paralysis and keeps us from achieving our goals.

Analysis paralysis is such a huge blockade that it becomes a never-ending downward spiral of self-sabotage and self-abuse. We are our own worst critics and often, if we are not careful, we can catch ourselves saying hurtful and destructive words to ourselves that we would never even tell our worst enemy.

It is important to understand how the different mindsets approach this fear, and how each of us can take on the mindset of the conqueror.

THE VICTIM MINDSET

The very first book I wrote, *The Game of Networking*, took me seven years to write.

I feared it wouldn't be good. Actually, it felt like I had ALL the fears included in *The Game of Networking* book!

I wanted it to be SO good that I just kept going and going. But even when it was done, it took two more years for it to actually come out and be published because of my fear of inadequacy.

Too many of us make a plan for the plan for the plan. We are so fearful of actually showing up and taking action. I was afraid of showing up and putting out my work. I played the victim for seven years as I continually told myself I wasn't enough. I thought that maybe if I just got one more quote. Maybe I needed to speak at one more live event to see how the audience would react. Again and again, there was always just a bit more prep work that needed to transpire before I could actually make the book happen.

I am so glad I showed up, wrote the book, and got it published. *The Game of Networking* has helped many people in learning important skills to improve their network marketing businesses. I let my fear stand in the way of helping others in my industry.

It took so long—not because I didn't work on it, and not because I didn't think about it—but because I wanted it to be perfect. The funny thing about the book is that it isn't perfect. It will never be perfect.

It was a great learning lesson for me. I learned that living in the fear of inadequacy just prolonged the outcome. The book you are reading right now took me less than nine months to write! I took action and realized I needed to take my own advice: "Do your best and forget the rest."

When it comes to the fear of inadequacy, victims live more inside their head than in the real world. It is their all-consuming thoughts, resting on their own inadequacies, that drive their behavior. And their behavior keeps them stuck in the same self-abusive cycle.

Victims who suffer from this fear isolate themselves. They either feel they are unworthy of the companionship of others, or they fear rejection is inevitable if others knew how inadequate they are. They close themselves off to others and the outside world because they fear that they have nothing to offer, or that what they do have to offer would offend others and dishearten the world around them.

Victims shut down opportunities for personal growth by not even entertaining the idea in the first place. Their lack of belief in themselves and their disbelief that they will ever be able to rise to the occasion keeps them from finding success. They are literally trapped in a world of their own making. Thoughts and beliefs are generated within their own mind. And those thoughts create fears and anxieties that shut them down.

If we are spiraling down into that paralyzing, debilitating way of living, there is always a way out. We just have to choose to overcome our fear of inadequacy and train our brain to think like a conqueror.

THE SURVIVOR MINDSET

When Gandhi was a young man, he was terrified of speaking. Although he was studying law, he felt great inadequacy in his ability to speak and influence others. It was a real weakness to him, and it impeded his capacity to succeed. On one occasion, Gandhi was invited to a popular London restaurant by the Vegetarian Society to give a speech on the overall benefits of living a vegetarian lifestyle.

Gandhi prepared his speech meticulously and even wrote it down so that all he had to do was read it in order to present it to members of the society. When it was time for his speech, Gandhi was only able to read one line before he was paralyzed with fear and could go no further. He handed his speech to someone else who read it and made the presentation for him.

Later, after Gandhi received his law degree, he set up a practice in London. But because of his fear of inadequacy in speaking, he was unable to find success, and his law practice failed. On one occasion, while in the courtroom, Gandhi was so paralyzed by his fear of speaking that he was unable to come up with a single question and ran out of the courtroom in cold sweats and embarrassment.

Think about that for a minute. Gandhi—who is known as one of the most powerful speakers and influencers of all time—allowed his fear of inadequacy to dictate his actions and it led to circumstances that spiraled down to a paralyzing, debilitating way of living. We will dive even more into Gandhi's story, but I want to point out right now that even the best of the best can succumb to the victim mindset.

After running the tennis club for four years, I felt capped out. The club was successful, but I wanted to be able to have the freedom to go on family vacations, live my life on purpose, and continue to make progress.

I started to buy all the entrepreneur magazines and read all the books on it I could find. I wanted to figure out what the next step would look like for me. I also used my networking skills to meet with many successful people and learned what their steps had been to reach the level they were at. After all of that, I was ready to make the leap to entrepreneurship.

I had never known anything except the tennis world. And because it was the only thing I knew, I didn't know how the transition into a completely different field would go.

A week into it, I decided to go all in on the new business venture. With the help of a mentor having more confidence in me than I had in myself, I decided to trust him. I went all in.

I quit my job one week in—which was too early, by the way!

The first month I did extremely well. But the second month wasn't as good. I was forced to go out and make some cold contacts, and I wasn't used to this. I 100 percent took the path of least resistance, which I knew wasn't the way.

I tried to do the "busy work" instead of doing the highest income producing activities.

The second month, I made $400. I also worked 80 hours every single week that month. But I was doing that checklist work. The busy work. And things started to spiral. I used more and more of my savings for our living expenses.

I had never been in debt in my life. I used up all our savings. One of our cars was paid off, which we were really proud of. Unfortunately, I had to go and get a loan on that car, which was completely humiliating for me. And, it gets worse.

We went from having a very comfortable lifestyle to living a basic needs lifestyle.

I had so many fears arise during this time. Fear of making the right decisions. Fear about this venture working out. Fear of quitting too soon. Fear about being able to provide for my family. But what it boiled down to was a fear of inadequacy. I was afraid I wouldn't be able to live up to the expectations of my wife and kids.

I didn't want this new venture to swallow me whole. I didn't want to go back to the tennis world. I wanted to see what was possible for me. But the real day-to-day pressure of providing for my family put me into survivor mode.

I lost my vision of the future because I couldn't see past my biggest fear of not being able to provide in the present. At one point, it got so bad that I started to play the credit card game. Many of you know what I am talking about. I was desperate to survive this time in our lives.

Some of my friends and family would ask me how my new business was going, and I wouldn't tell them what was really going on. I didn't want them to know how much we were struggling. I didn't want people to see me as weak. I didn't want them to think I had made a mistake leaving the tennis club.

I can remember one moment, in particular, when I was in complete despair. I had so much shame I didn't even want to talk to my wife about it. I felt I couldn't rely on anyone else—I had to face my demons. I didn't want to JUST survive anymore.

Survivors recognize they have inadequacies, but they don't want others to know. Instead, they'll brag about what they can do and what they are good at in order to remove the focus from what they can't do. Many times, this leads to overcompensation…and a big ego.

They may also rationalize and compare, seeking and exposing the inadequacies of others, to help them feel better about their own. They are constantly—yet often unconsciously—looking for reasons why they are better than those around them. They seek to build themselves up, often by putting others down, in order to make themselves look better.

Survivor mindset will say things like, "Well, at least I'm not like that person. I'm much better at (xyz) than they are!" Without even knowing it, survivors will surround themselves with people they feel are less adequate than they are. That way, they'll always have someone to compare their life to and come out the winner.

When they do manage to meet someone who they esteem as greater than themselves—someone who is popular in the eyes of others— survivors will often try to align themselves with this person. Not to learn from them, but to use their association with the person as a status symbol, and a claim to fame for themselves.

Survivors will use comparison with popular people as well, but the comparison always puts the popular person and the survivor in the same category. Even if they are lacking, a survivor will seek to boast about their inadequacies in such a way that they are perceived as strengths when compared to someone great. They can claim that they are almost as good as the popular person, and therefore increase their own status in the eyes of others.

Rather than working to turn their weaknesses into strengths, survivors are happy to simply ride on the coattails of others. And to help themselves feel better, survivors will rationalize why it's okay if they don't succeed, without taking responsibility for their part in their own success. They are so busy compensating for their weaknesses that they never grow in strength. They simply survive. Unless they take that next step, they will never conquer.

It is said that comparison is the thief of joy. Whether we are comparing ourselves to someone great and robbing ourselves of our own joy, or proving we are better than others and stealing their joy, either way, we become thieves, not conquerors. Conquerors don't steal joy, they seek to share it.

How many times do we, as survivors, self-sabotage our success because we are so focused on hiding our weaknesses or justifying them? We never let our weaknesses become strengths. We step back, never really putting our heart into the game, because we are scared, don't feel we deserve more, or we are simply content with just being in the game. Because of our beliefs, we put no extra effort into actually winning.

How many times do we settle in life for being average or even just good? We use our fear of being inadequate to stop us from really stepping into greatness.

How many times do we shrink our dreams, goals, and ambitions to make ourselves and others feel comfortable? We all have inadequacies and weaknesses. That is simply part of mortality. But it is what we do with those weaknesses that define us. I truly believe that every weakness can be turned into a strength. We just need to accept the challenge and change our mindset to that of a conqueror.

THE CONQUEROR MINDSET

Even conquerors have inadequacies. But it is how they view their inadequacies that makes them a conqueror. The conqueror realizes that success can only come from daily intentional and a positive outlook on life. They use the Conqueror's Formula to intentionally see their inadequacies and work them into strengths. They are creators and thus create their own success by focusing on the things they can do and by developing the courage to do those things, even when it becomes difficult. It's not that they don't have fears—they absolutely do. But they are able to train their brain to push past their fears and to find a motivation that is stronger than those fears that keep most people prisoners.

Conquerors are able to take a step back and look at the bigger picture. Once they do, they realize that success in life is not about them, it is about serving other people by choosing to be the good in the world. Their world is much bigger than they are. Their desire is to help the whole human race by bringing what goodness they can to the table. Their focus is on what they can do, not in being perfect. And because of this, they can push through just about anything and create a better world for themselves and for everyone around them.

The incredible thing about all of this is that we can all become conquerors! We don't have to stay in that victim or survivor mindset. With just a few vital changes in our thinking, we can be a conqueror and bring good to the world.

When I left the tennis club and was struggling in network marketing, I was able to eventually rise from being a survivor to a conqueror and find a lot of success within that field. The first step I had to take was to accept **COMPLETE** responsibility for everything. All of it. I didn't shrink away from my weaknesses, I didn't hide in shame from my wife. I took ownership and was able to work up the ladder of success from there.

Now, let's go back to Gandhi. As a young lawyer, he felt defeated. He struggled so much in those early years after law school that he closed his practice in London and moved back to his native land in India. While in India, he saw the injustices of the world and decided that he couldn't sit back and watch people suffer without doing something.

Gandhi began speaking out, even though it was hard, and even when it scared him. Because what scared him even more was that no one was speaking up and he was watching people suffer in silence.

Gandhi's cause was greater than himself, and greater than the fear of public speaking that had kept him silent. It was his cause that pushed him out of his comfort zone and right past his fear of inadequacy. By pushing past that fear, Gandhi became one of the greatest influencers this world has ever known. Not only was his audience filled with freedom fighters, politicians, philosophers, and scholars, but he reached out to the poor, the needy, the vagrant, and the pauper. He was a man of the people and the people still speak of him in hushed and reverent tones for the good he did—not just for India, but for the world.

Gandhi is the perfect example to teach us that our fears do not have to define us and that we do not have to live in the victim and survivor mentality. It is a choice. And once we make the choice to be a conqueror, our inadequacies can become our strengths and our greatest lessons can be learned from them.

Gandhi said, "My hesitancy in speech, which was once an annoyance, is now a pleasure. Its greatest benefit has been that it has taught me the economy of words."

What a powerful lesson Gandhi received from what once was an inadequacy he feared. Great lessons like this can come to us too, if we let them.

If Gandhi's story isn't enough to inspire you, let me share my own.

Like Gandhi, I also feared public speaking. As I become more deliberate in improving my public speaking, I went through many struggles—learning hard lessons and having challenging experiences. But now, that so-called weakness is one of my greatest strengths.

As I shifted into sales, I knew I would need to get better at speaking. At age 28, I made a decision that changed my life. You see, success truly does start in the mind and in the choices we make.

I decided that I would take every opportunity I was given to speak in front of people. I would push myself through the struggle. After I spoke, I would look for feedback on how I could improve. I began to study speakers—their style, word choice, tone, posture, and delivery. I bought books to learn more about public speaking. And I didn't just read the books, I actually applied what I learned. I went out and I made a deliberate choice to speak, even when it was hard.

I would speak to small groups by presenting my sales pitch as often as possible. I asked and looked for opportunities to speak to anyone and everyone. I failed forward!

During my first big conference call, there were over 1,000 people looking for training. My mentor at the time had me present a training to the salesforce for about ten minutes. After the training, my mentor asked me how I thought I had done. I said that on a scale from 1 to 10, I believed I was about a 7.

Now to give you context, my mentor had been wildly successful and was brutally honest. We had been good friends for years and he never sugarcoated anything. He then proceeded to tell me that on a scale from 1 to 10, my presentation was a 1 and I sounded like I was at my father's funeral. He said I was monotone and boring. I still remember laughing out loud—almost crying.

My mentor said over the phone, "Are you laughing right now?"

I responded, "Yes! I can't believe I was that bad!"

He then proceeded to tell me that I was going to do great things because I was so coachable and willing to go through hard times. After three years, I had become the #1 recruiter in the company for new sales—a company that had about a million other sales representatives!

I still wasn't great at public speaking, but I was much better. It took me a good seven years to become pretty good at public speaking. Seven years!

And now, I have found great success with what I felt was one of my biggest inadequacies. I have now spoken to audiences of over 10,000. I have spoken in 16 different countries, and I have my own motivational events all over the world. I have been able to reach out and touch thousands of people's lives with an inadequacy that continued to stare me in the face when I was younger.

The incredible thing in life is that sometimes, what we perceive as an inadequacy is actually one of our greatest strengths in its early stages of development. And if we choose to learn and develop that weakness, it can change our life. I am so passionate about this particular topic of public speaking that I have created a FREE video training all on public speaking **www.sperrybonus.com**. This training will help you to become a better communicator and trainer and increase your sponsoring.

I get paid a lot of money to do that one thing I once felt most inadequate to do. Through making the decision to learn about and develop that weakness, I have become one of the top speakers in the world. Of course, I am not world-renowned like Tony Robbins, but based on how much I get paid per speech, I am in the top few percent of speakers out there. It still humbles me when I think about how far I have come.

When it comes to the fear of inadequacy, it was that one decision that I made that became the turning point for me. And every decision I have made, every day after that, has supported and strengthened that decision. It really is the decisions we make every single day that form our habits and allow us to push past our fears to become a conqueror.

HOW TO CONQUER FEAR OF INADEQUACY

A person can increase their success by up to 95 percent through fostering good habits and weeding out the bad. With good habits put in place, anyone can gain the knowledge and the necessary skill set to turn their weakness into a strength. And with the right habits, accompanied by the right mindset, success is bound to happen.

As mentioned earlier in the Conqueror Formula, it has been said by many researchers that, on average, we make 35,000 decisions every single day. Most of those decisions don't feel like decisions because we don't really even think about them. They are simply habits that have been developed.

To become a conqueror and strengthen our weaknesses, we need to first strengthen our habits. Most studies believe that habits take at least

28 days to form. Which, in the whole scheme of things, doesn't sound like a lot, and it shouldn't be too hard to do. And yet, we all struggle to form those good habits that will benefit us and to let go of those bad habits that are keeping us stuck.

To help you in your efforts to create good habits that will allow you to strengthen your inadequacies and overcome your fears, here are a few things I have done to help me stay focused.

Over a decade ago, I started out with a printed excel spreadsheet that many now call their DMO, or Daily Method of Operation. I had it organized into categories, with a box next to each category to check it off once it was accomplished. Some of those categories stayed the same, while others would change depending on what my focus and goals were at that time.

For example, here are a few categories I had: Working out for at least 45 minutes, prayers, studying personal development, studying something spiritual, date night once a week with my wife, food goals, and then many other business goals which would change frequently.

I would check all of these off each time I accomplished them. I put the spreadsheet in my room or in my bathroom to make it visual because I wanted to see it every day.

Earlier in the book I gave you an update of what results I have gotten by setting my goals and having dedicated time. You may want to make that same goal. What it really goes back to is setting up your own Conqueror's Formula and taking action from it. Do you have a defined vision? Have you set up an environment to support your vision? Are you showing up daily with discipline? Are you sticking to your habits?

Do a daily check in at the end of the day with the Conqueror's Formula as your guide. The more you follow the formula, the more success you will create.

I know I am not naturally the best at virtually anything. I'm sure that I am very inadequate compared to others in most things. But how I win is that I out-discipline others. I create strong habits and I stick to them. These habits create my future.

I no longer have a spreadsheet for any of those main things. Why? Because they are all habits now.

You can create habits, just like that. And when you do, you will also see success. Here are some tips that will help you.

- **DECLARE *WHAT* YOU REALLY WANT.** Most people don't know what they really want, and they aren't specific enough. Be specific! Go back to the Conqueror's Formula and fill in the vision you would like to create for your life.

- **DECLARE *WHY* YOU REALLY WANT IT.** Remember, your why has to be stronger than your mood swings. Why do you want your specific goal? Create the habits that will help you achieve your goals.

- **MAKE IT VISUAL.** Put your goals up someplace so they're visual. Place your DMOs wherever you can see them every day. Create a dream board that has pictures of your goals. Look at your goals often.

- **SET REMINDERS ON YOUR PHONE.** Have different alarms that go off every day with different sayings to keep you focused on your goals. Intentionally create the sayings that will help move you above and through your inadequacy.

- **BE ACCOUNTABLE.** Accountability accelerates your performance. The American Society of Training and Development (ASTD) did a study on accountability and found that you have a 65 percent greater chance of completing a goal if you commit to someone. And if you have a specific accountability appointment with a person to whom you've committed, you will increase your chances of success by up to 95 percent. So, find someone that you can be accountable with and create a set of appointments.

These are some ideas I have found that help me keep the conqueror mindset and overcome my fear of inadequacy. There are so many ways to create good habits in your life. Find the tools that work for you and get started on turning those paralyzing weaknesses into your greatest strengths.

HOW TO CREATE STRONG HABITS

√ Declare **what** you really want

√ Declare **why** you really want it

√ Make it visual

√ Set reminders on your phone

√ Be accountable

"FOMO lures us out of our integrity with whispers about what we could or should be doing. FOMO's favorite weapon is comparison."

-Brene Brown

CHAPTER 8

MISSING OUT

Michael Jackson is one of the most iconic singers of our time. He was brought up singing in the family band and later went on to become a successful solo artist. Despite his successful career, his personal life was severely affected and altered from having a deep fear of missing out.

He grew up in the spotlight as the bright and bubbly younger brother in the Jackson 5. He got to have experiences that most kids didn't, but what he really wanted was a normal childhood. Michael would see other kids playing in parks, hanging out with friends and family, and he would have a deep yearning to have that type of life.

When Michael became an adult, he felt he had missed out on a huge part of his life. He had a fear of missing his childhood because of working at such a young age. He spent the rest of his lifetime trying to recreate what he thought his childhood should have been.

The fear of missing out, also known as FOMO, may have only been in the Oxford Dictionary since 2016, but the fear has been around for ages.

I would bet that almost everyone experienced this fear very early on in their childhood. It may have reared its ugly head the moment you learned you were not invited to a birthday party, or when you noticed that "everyone" had a certain pair of shoes. Everyone, that is, except you.

The fear of missing out is a fear that comes when we believe others are having better experiences than we are. We falsely believe people are happier because they own bigger and better cars and houses, because they are taking more extravagant vacations, and because they have an all-around better life.

The sad truth is that at one time or another, most of us have been overly preoccupied by the belief that somewhere, there is someone who is having more fun, raking in more money, or living a more exciting and fulfilling life than we are. And because of this preoccupation, we stop living our own lives because we are too busy fantasizing about someone else's.

Social media has only increased this fear by expanding our ability to see and explore an endless supply of other people's lives with a simple flick of the finger. And instead of being centered and involved and present in the physical world around us, many people turn their time and attention to social media outlets in order to search out the happiness of other people.

I love how much social media has enhanced many aspects of the network marketing profession. It is a great way to find new potential customers and distributors. It has so many benefits that have helped the profession. But all strengths have massive weaknesses.

One massive weakness with social media and network marketing is that network marketers are having FOMO from other network marketing companies. They are seeing the perfect highlights of one's success in another network marketing company. And they mistakenly start to believe that the issue isn't themselves, but it must be the company they are in.

I have seen more people switching companies because of this than ever before. I am not, by any means, saying one shouldn't switch companies (that's a personal decision for each individual). But what I am saying is that I believe many people switch companies way too soon and way too often because of this social media FOMO effect.

Unhappiness is the number one driver of FOMO. We all seek happiness. And many times, when we are unhappy in our own lives, we seek that happiness in the lives of others. When we see our friends and associates experiencing joy, we want what they have. We think if only we could be somewhere else, doing something else, with someone else, we could be happy. But if we can't do that, we stalk people on social media, living vicariously through them, so that we can learn the key to their happiness and make it our own.

Even worse than stalking happy people is trying to be just like them. Oftentimes, unhappy people will see the physical possessions that happy people have, and they will waste all of their money buying those things, thinking that it will bring them happiness. Happiness does not come from other people, places, or things.

This "keeping up with the Joneses" approach is rampant in our society today because we live in a world of comparison. Many people seek to be the "king of the hill," and win the imaginary prize. They want to be on top, with the biggest and the best of everything. They don't want to just be happy—they want to be happier than everyone else. It's as if happiness were finite and they want the biggest slice of the pie.

Montesquieu, a 1700 French philosopher, said this about happiness:

"If one only wished to be happy, this could be easily accomplished; but we wish to be happier than other people, and this is always difficult, for we believe others to be happier than they are."

Let's stop and put it all in perspective for a moment. Think back to hundreds of years ago. Imagine if you were a king or queen. You would have more than anyone else. Now fast forward to the present. How much higher is your quality of living versus a king or queen? You have so many possessions that were not even available to kings and queens.

We can travel and see the world. We have amazing transportation through airplanes and automobiles that didn't even exist back then. We have knowledge at our fingertips because we live in the Information Age. Hundreds of years ago, if you traveled for months or years away from loved ones, there would be little to no communication. Now, not only do we have calling and texting, but we can communicate via videos. I could go on and on, but you catch my point.

We live better than kings and queens. And yet we don't feel like it. We attempt to create happiness based on what we have that others don't. That is not happiness. It is a false measurement that only causes more confusion as to why we still aren't truly happy. There will always be someone who has more than you. Always!

One of my favorite sayings is, "It is impossible to be grateful and unhappy at the same time."

We need to remember the fear of missing out drives us to believe that others are happier than they portray. And even though we are mostly aware that the photos and posts on social media are edited versions of real life, we choose to step into that world and away from our own to search out greater happiness. In doing that, we miss out on the opportunity to live our own life and create our own happiness.

People who struggle with FOMO are caught in a cycle that will never change, until they change their way of thinking. Those who have the fear of missing out spend their days looking outward for their happiness, instead of looking within. They have failed to learn that happiness isn't in things or experiences—it is in us.

The fear of missing out is a fear experienced by even the best of us. But how we approach the fear determines whether we are a victim, survivor, or conqueror. The only way to face the fear and overcome it is to learn how to see it from the eyes of a conqueror.

THE VICTIM MINDSET

A member of *The Game of Networking* Facebook group shared an experience with me. She had a goal of qualifying for her company's top earner cruise. Unfortunately, she had missed it by just a bit. She was devastated! She had such a big fear of missing out on the cruise and not being able to spend time with the company executives and other top earners of the company. She was so upset about what she was missing that she didn't recognize all she had done. She didn't build on the momentum that she had gained trying to earn the trip. She just stopped doing anything in her business.

The week of the cruise, she obsessively checked social media to see what was happening and what everyone was enjoying. She felt jealous and left out. Her dear friend, who was on the trip, noticed the "poor me" attitude she was posting in the comments of everyone's pictures. The friend messaged her and said, "We wish you were here, but this type of attitude isn't going to get you here next year! Drop the drama and get to work!!"

I love that advice.

To be part of my mastermind group, members must make and maintain a six- or seven-figure income. People message me all the time wanting to be "a fly on the wall" during our mastermind retreats.

"Rob, can you stream just ONE presentation from the mastermind?"
"Rob, can you SHARE your notes from the mastermind?"

Get to work and you can join the mastermind and take your own notes at the retreats. I know that's tough love but this whole book is meant to get you into action to help you achieve those goals you have!

Victims are so focused on what others have that they are unable to bring their own life into focus. They become watchers rather than doers, always wanting but never achieving an authentic life of happiness. This kind of behavior becomes a distraction and stops good people from being the good in the world. Instead, they take a back seat to the successes of others and allow their life to slowly slip by them, unknown and unhappy.

Because social media is such a huge part of the world today, it is easy to get sucked into other people's lives and enter that cycle of FOMO. I am sure we have all suffered from the fear of missing out, at one time or another, as we have perused those perfectly posed pictures. But it is equally as easy to get ourselves out of it by simply unplugging ourselves and stepping into our own lives.

Being a victim of anything is a choice we make. Being a conqueror is also a choice.

Just as there are different levels of survivors and conquerors, there are different levels of victims. The next few paragraphs are meant to be extreme on purpose. I will give you a detailed view of an extreme victim to illustrate the dangers that can and do happen.

Victims are not active in creating the life they desire. They want something different but want someone else to give it to them. Oftentimes, victims can be found tucked away staring at their screens. They scroll for hours consuming posts and pictures of people, places, and things they wish they had. FOMO hits hard as they continue to see what they don't have.

Victims will live their lives vicariously through the characters of books, movies, or people they follow on social media. They long to have love and adventure and are afraid that they are missing out on the world, so they insert themselves into other people's lives, even the made-up ones! I once heard two people describe a popular reality TV family as if it were their own family. They talked about an entire episode as if it were their OWN reality they were discussing. Binge-watching movies and television gives them the life they fear they are missing out on, and it becomes their new way of living. Entertainment is no longer a casual thing for them, but a coping mechanism for unhappiness.

Because they are so busy minding other people's business, their own business never goes anywhere because no one is minding it.

THE SURVIVOR MINDSET

I love to go on trips and find adventure. My wife and I love seeing the world. We really wanted to go to Kauai and go on a specific hike on the Napali Coast. The hike is 22 miles and requires you to camp overnight. Anytime we told people we were going to Kauai they would gush about how amazing this hike was. We even had people tell us that it was a once-in-a-lifetime experience. Both of us didn't want to miss out on this experience, but 22 miles and camping didn't really appeal to us.

Our friend told us about a way to get dropped off on the beach at the end of the hike. Then we would hike the 11 miles out, and there would be no need to camp. We decided that sounded perfect for us.

We showed up at some random guy's house that would be dropping us off at the hike. We wanted to go on a boat but found out it wasn't available. This guy was ranting and raving about his jet ski not working. He was fuming as he tried to fix the jet ski. Now, because the boat wasn't an option, this was the only guy and the only jet ski that was going to take us to our destination. At that point, I was pretty hesitant. I kept glancing at my wife with wide eyes and motioning her with a head tilt that maybe we should go. As he worked on his jet ski, he mentioned that the swells in the ocean were 15 PLUS feet that day.

I don't know about you, but that has always been scary to me. I really questioned if this was a good idea.

He finally got the jet ski running and told us that we needed to hurry to get out before the waves got worse.

I was freaking out! And those who know me know that I rarely ever freak out! As he put the jet ski in the ocean, I looked out and could see that 100 feet out from the shore there were these HUGE swells. The three of us hopped onto the SAME jet ski and took off into the waves.

Crazy jet ski guy timed his entry into the swells perfectly, and we made it through the first group of swells. He yelled at us that the worst was behind us, but I didn't believe it. He had us riding the crest of these waves. It is basically the top of the wave and we were looking down at the bottom of the ocean.

I kept thinking that if we crash, we were going to die.

All this time that I am freaking out in my head about crashing and dying, my wife was having her own freak-out about sharks. She is very afraid of sharks. She was sitting there, riding this jet ski, and terrified to even see a shark swimming near her.

Why would both of us get on some random guy's clunky jet ski in treacherous conditions?

We didn't want to miss out. We justified all of this and decided to survive because our fear of missing out was so big. I had this thought that if we went home without doing this hike, we wouldn't have REALLY done Kauai. And, of course, if we didn't get that perfect shot for Instagram, no one would know that we had done Kauai the right way! In hindsight, we put ourselves at unnecessary risk for the wrong reason. By the way, the hike was epic and totally worth it.

Typically, the fear of missing out leads us to believe that the grass is greener on the other side of the fence, and we long to be there. So, we consume our lives with that quest. But in reality, the grass is only greener on the other side because the grass on the other side has been watered. It has been nurtured and when something is nurtured, it grows. If you want green grass, water your own lawn—nurture your own dreams, and stop yearning for the dreams of others. Because when you are consumed with the lives of others, it is your own life that you are really missing out on.

It is difficult for anyone to stay positive when they are comparing other people's edited versions of life to their own sad life. So, when a survivor sees someone with more, what do you think they do? They create their own post. To compensate for what they lack, they brag about what they have, or even make up what they don't have. I witnessed a woman on a beach scream at her kids to create the perfect picture of their family enjoying their vacation. After she got the picture, the woman didn't interact with her kids for the rest of the day. She may have gotten the "Insta-worthy" shot, but it wasn't real life. It was a fake photo, for the fake life that she wanted everyone else to see as her reality. It may have been what she wanted for her life, but she wasn't willing to show up and create the actual experience with her family. This mindset just adds to the problem and creates FOMO in someone else viewing their post.

If a friend posts a picture of something exciting, the survivor will seek out something equally exciting in their own life to post or blow something up to be grander than it is, to one-up their friends. The survivor will take 100 selfies, just to find the one perfect pose to post to their friends. Okay, I may be exaggerating the number of selfies they take, but not by much. Survivors are consumed with perfection, and quite often the perfect picture is the only picture they will allow their friends to see. Don't freak out over this. Of course, there are many times when it is okay to take multiple shots to get a great photo. But I am talking about the person who ALWAYS has to take 100 selfies for just about every photo.

The difference between a victim and a survivor when it comes to FOMO is that a survivor will go out and do. A survivor is pro-active and makes things happen. Someone with a victim mindset will just sit by and watch and wish but won't go out and do anything.

Social media allows the survivor to keep up the appearance of perfection, while not actually having to be perfect. We know that no one is perfect, but social media has a way of making us believe that being perfect is a real thing—and that happiness comes with perfection. So, we strive to catch that elusive happiness.

Survivors are those who will go into serious debt just to buy a bigger boat, a bigger house, or a bigger car in order to prove that they are living the perfectly happy life worth emulating. Their FOMO is so large that they will do anything to prove they are living the life of their dreams and that others are the ones missing out.

As I said before, survivors are never satisfied with what they have because there is always someone out there who is living a better life than they are. They are ever searching for and never finding their own happiness. Like the victim, they are left wanting and their way of compensating is to accumulate more, believing more will finally make them happy.

THE CONQUEROR MINDSET

In 2008, when I first really grasped this concept, I gave up TV entirely for six months and focused on launching my network marketing business. I did this because I wanted to create more wealth, which would create more time to make a greater impact. I also gave up watching the NFL on Sundays to spend more time with my family.

That same year, I also decided to give up listening to music at the gym. Instead, I listened to personal development books. Of course, it was hard, but I wanted to focus on becoming a better leader, father, husband, and businessman. Instead of telling myself I was missing out on listening to fun music, and getting pumped up during my workout, I told myself I was gaining something even better. The conqueror mindset has made all the difference.

If your focus is on what you think you've lost, or what you feel you can't have, you are going to make yourself miserable. You are always going to find yourself wanting, because you will be wanting what you are telling yourself you can't have.

But, if you tell yourself that you are choosing to give up something you like for something you love even more, the sacrifice isn't as hard. Music is something I find a pleasure and I enjoy listening to it. But my love and dedication to bettering myself was greater than the desire for music. When you are focused on the good that will come from it—and not the sacrifice itself—hope becomes your motivation, and with hope, you can accomplish anything. There really is power in a positive

THE GAME OF CONQUERING

attitude, so focus on the good and stop thinking about what you're
missing out on.

Please don't misinterpret the principles I am teaching. Don't go and get
panicked thinking I am telling you that you can't or shouldn't listen to
music. Everyone has their outlets. For me it has always been movies.
No matter how focused I was, my wife and I would always make
time to watch movies late at night. This was my outlet where I could
recharge my batteries. Music may be that for you.

The conqueror may suffer from FOMO, but their approach is a much
healthier approach than the victim or the survivor. The conqueror may
long for a bigger house, or faster car, but rather than live vicariously
through others, or go into large amounts of debt for the sake of
appearance, they work for it. Work ethic is a valuable skill set for the
conqueror.

While victims are dreaming and survivors are pretending, conquerors
are working hard to make their dreams a reality. Conquerors have a
vision of what they want, where they are going, and understand the
work it will take to get there. They make plans, set goals, and create a
vision board to make things happen. They focus on what they can do,
not what they want—which allows them to get exactly what they want
in the end.

When a conqueror focuses on what they want, they do not see it as
something they can't have, nor do they feel that it's something they are
lacking. They see it as something attainable with a little hard work and
with their eyes fixated on the prize.

Conquerors are able to reframe how they see things and the story they
tell themselves, in order to make meaningful things happen in their life.
When they see someone with something they want, they ask themselves
what it would take for them to get there. Then they make a plan and
get to work. In their efforts to reach their goals, they are willing to give

up the things they like in order to attain something they might love even more.

While others are incapable of giving up their television or video games because of their fear of missing out, conquerors voluntarily give up those things in order to create their own authentic life of happiness.

Often, I will encourage people to ask themselves this question: "Am I hanging on to too many likes, which are preventing me from my loves?" What does this mean? Too many of us confuse our likes with our loves. We mix the two together. Conquerors understand the difference between the two. You may like watching five hours of TV a day, but you love being able to travel the world with your family. If you hang onto all your likes, you won't ever gain those loves. You must give up something smaller to gain something bigger. I will give you more in-depth tips on this shortly.

Often, with FOMO, people are enthralled with social media and entertainment because it fills a void for them and temporarily makes them happy. But what they don't understand is that the happiness that comes from real-life relationships and accomplishments far outweighs any happiness they can receive from virtual living. Yet they won't give up virtual reality for something better. FOMO keeps people holding onto imaginary lives and edited photos that never truly bring them a life that they love.

HOW TO CONQUER FOMO

Here is an exercise for you: List what you like in life and, in a separate column, list what you love. Most of us aren't willing to give up likes—such as TV and social media—to gain what we love. In the end, by obsessing over the things that we like, our loves—such as more time and freedom with our family—are never attained.

Again, don't freak out! Look, I am not saying to give up all your likes—but I am saying that if you want to go from a victim or survivor to a conqueror, you'll need to make sacrifices. And you'll need to be okay with missing out on things that aren't really a benefit to you anyway. Kobe Bryant said, "We can all be masters at our craft, but you have to make sacrifices that come along with making that decision."

We need to listen to ourselves less and talk to ourselves more. Our minds can naturally be negative. To combat our nature and negative self-talk, we need to stop listening to ourselves talk that negative talk, and instead, give ourselves a positive pep-talk. We have all heard the phrase, "Look on the bright side." This isn't just something nice we say to one another, it really works. Positive psychology has actually proven that resilience stems from the ability to see the good.

Living a life of happiness also comes from learning to be grateful for what you already have. When you are grateful for what you have, you don't fear what you're missing out on. What you are missing out on won't even matter, because gratitude makes what you have enough. Then striving and working for more becomes healthy and positive. You are working for the right reasons.

Don't just hear this advice—but implement it. If you are struggling in any aspect of your network marketing business, go all out on a gratitude binge. List everything you are grateful for in your business. Turn those trials into gratitude learning lessons.

Before I give you a few ideas that will help you with your FOMO, understand that I am not bashing on social media. I actually love social media. I have slowly unfriended or unfollowed anyone who doesn't add value to my life. I don't believe social media really adds anything to our lives. I think social media reveals to us all our insecurities. Just like money, social media will make you more of what you already are. With that said, some of us need to take extreme measures while we are learning to do deal with our FOMO.

Here are some ideas to help you conquer FOMO and live the authentic happy life that you deserve.

- **KEEP A GRATITUDE JOURNAL.** When you are grateful for what you have, your desire for more is greatly diminished. What you focus on grows.

- **UNPLUG.** The best way to squash FOMO is to step away from social media. Go for a walk, do something kind for someone else, spend time with your family. When you unplug, you are better able to appreciate what you already have.

- **GO ON A SOCIAL MEDIA/TV/ELECTRONICS FAST.** When I stopped watching TV, I was amazed at all I was able to accomplish. My productivity sky-rocketed and my business flourished.

- **BE GENUINELY HAPPY FOR OTHERS AND THEIR ACCOMPLISHMENTS.** It will diminish your ego when you put your focus on others instead of yourself.

- **CREATE YOUR OWN HAPPINESS.** Spend time each day meditating on your happy place and learn to generate your happiness from within.

- **MAKE A PLAN.** Construct a vision board of your hopes and dreams, make a plan of how to achieve them—then get to work.

FOMO may have stopped you from moving forward in the past, but you don't have to let it dictate how you live your life now. Happiness is real and it is attainable. Success in your network marketing business is attainable. Change your focus—change your business. Change your focus—change your life. The way to attain the happiness you seek is easier than you may think. Stop looking at the green grass on the other side and start watering your own lawn. Because in your fear of missing out, it is your own life you are missing out on.

"Out of a fear of the unknown, people prefer suffering that is familiar."

-Nhat Hanh

CHAPTER 9

UNKNOWN

What would our world be like if explorers would have given in to their fear of the unknown? Can you imagine if Christopher Columbus had a victim or survivor mindset when he set off to explore and discover? Explorers are literally facing the unknown as they seek new knowledge about the unexplored.

Edmund Hillary was the first man to summit Mount Everest. At the time, Nepal was only allowing one to two groups a year to hike in the area. Edmund never knew if he would get the chance to even take a crack at the summit. So, when he heard that he had been accepted, he couldn't let the fear of the unknown stop him from accomplishing his dream. Edmund said after his epic summit, "It is not the mountain we conquer, but ourselves."

I personally am so grateful for early explorers who didn't let the fear of the unknown stop them from discovering something new and different. My ancestors left everything they had to walk across the plains of the

United States and settle in a completely unknown place. When they started their trek, they didn't even know where they were going!

The vast majority of human beings value the ability to be in control. Being in control is viewed as a positive trait. Because of this, fear of the unknown is a persistent trait experienced by many. We long to be in control of our life and circumstances. We pride ourselves, and are admired by others, when we are in control of any given situation. We wear being in control as a badge of honor for all to see.

Fear of the unknown, in its greatest simplicity, is fear of anything that is outside of our own comfort zone. Many of us fear the unknown because we can't easily and fully anticipate the outcome. Even our brains are hardwired for this way of thinking. It has actually been proven that our brain prefers negative consequences that are predictable over outcomes that are uncertain. How crazy is that?! Our nature is to STAY in a bad situation rather than try something new or different that has the potential to be great.

The truth is, no matter how hard we try, we cannot control circumstances. We talked about that earlier in this book. Circumstances are outside of us. This leads some people to resist circumstances changing in their lives. Have you ever heard the saying, "Whatever we resist, persists?" Not only is this true, but it is certain. Resisting change makes things more difficult in the long run and keeps us from progressing. We remain dormant inside of our comfort zone, making choices that are easy, in order to avoid something hard. We strive to lessen the unknown and keep things within our control.

We need to train our mind to step back, look at the big picture, and embrace the unknown. When we do this, we can make better choices—choices that will lead us outside of our comfort zone and into a place where we can grow.

Change is risky and uncertain for all of us. But, as it is with all other fears, it is how we choose to look at change, and how we approach the unknown, that determines whether we are a victim, survivor, or conqueror.

THE VICTIM MINDSET

I remember when I started out in network marketing, I had some great success the first couple of months, but I also had a ton of failure. I didn't know when success was coming. I didn't know IF it would come. It felt like success was the luck of the draw and not something that you could intentionally create. I was so afraid of what my luck would bring. I was afraid of the unknown. I was so afraid of the unknown that I started blaming everyone else. I started looking at others who were successful and saying, "The only reason they found success is they found the right person. They found the superstar." I would see another person and think, "They are in a really good area." "They joined at the exact right time." I like to call these types of excuses the "yeah, but…" excuses. "Yeah, they are successful, BUT it is because…"

What it came down to was my own insecurities. I had a fear of not knowing. If I would have known that success would come two years from that time, or even FIVE years from that time, it would have made all the difference for me. It was the unknown that created all the doubts and insecurities. The fear of the unknown led me to become the victim. I stopped taking 100 percent accountability of my own actions.

Stop and think about this: How does the fear of the unknown affect you? If you knew for sure that whatever success you desire would come to you in three years, guaranteed, if you made three new contacts every day, how would that change your daily actions?

Fear of the unknown is a major hindrance to progression when a person is in the victim mindset. Victims fear that the future will be just like the past. They fear making decisions when the possibility of the outcome could be more of the same trial they have already experienced. Even when their circumstances are less than desirable, victims prefer staying in their comfort zone because it is what they know—rather than taking a leap of faith into something uncertain. They continue to hold themselves back from a decision that also has the potential of being something good.

In every choice we make, there is a chance that we will either win or lose. But because victims are afraid of the loss, they never make the choice, and in doing this, they keep themselves from the win. In essence, they sabotage themselves from ever achieving something great and continue to live inside their comfort zone.

I have learned that choosing to focus on the negative possibilities based on past negative experiences is what keeps us a victim of our past. I allowed my perceived negative experience from a young teenager hold me hostage and did everything to protect me from those fears. What experiences do you have a negative perspective on that have caused you to have fears? Which fears have held you hostage? I want you to think. Think of all your insecurities. Think of all your so-called weaknesses. What specific experiences did you have that you could now look back on and see as a positive learning experience?

THE SURVIVOR MINDSET

As I shifted from the victim to the survivor, the fear of the unknown didn't change. It just wasn't as big. I started to take more responsibility, created a bit more success, took more action, and focused on the solution. Even still, I was held back. I was showing up to meetings, team trainings, and having team calls. I would reach out to team members, work on personal development, and set goals. What I was doing was FAKE-WORKING. The fear of the unknown kept me from going all in. I wanted the success, but I didn't know if it would ever happen for me.

I wanted to be all in. I told people I was all in. But my actions, weren't all in. I kept avoiding the #1 income producing activity. I wasn't reaching out to brand new people. I would do EVERYTHING else. I would make the checklist with twenty items on it and I would get it all done—except for reaching out to new people.

As a side note, I hope you have already downloaded my full list of the income producing activities at **www.sperrybonus.com**. Print it out and put it somewhere you can see it every day. Don't do what I did. Start by doing these income producing activities from the very beginning.

In my own business efforts, I was the one who was taking the path of least resistance. I was doing the fake work. It was too scary to go all in with doing a business filled with the unknown. What if I did go all in, and it didn't give me success? I learned something about being a survivor through this experience. Just surviving is exhausting.

What you choose to focus on and how you perceive every moment of your past and present will dictate what your future will be. If you choose to act, you will be progressing and deciding your future. And most of the time, even when the outcome may be scary, you will realize that more often than not, when the unknown becomes known, there was nothing to be afraid of after all.

A survivor's fear of the unknown is not in their circumstances, but in themselves and their ability to make a better choice. Survivor's often take responsibility for their circumstances, but they still lack faith in themselves to change their future. They typically do not have the fear that the past will repeat itself, but their fear is that they will repeat the same mistakes over and over again.

Survivors are living on the line between comfort and possibility, trying to stand firmly in both worlds. They have hope in the possibilities of the future, but they struggle to take action because of their past mistakes.

The only way a survivor can progress is by taking action steps every day while keeping their focus on what lies directly in front of them.

One of the best analogies I can give survivors to aid in their perspective of progress is the shadow vs the sun analogy.

The sun represents progress. When you are headed towards the sun—whether that be crawling, walking, jogging or running—you are happy. You are progressing towards your vision. And you are successfully progressing towards your goal.

But the second you stop moving forward, and make the choice to look behind you, you see your shadow—which represents your mistakes. Immediately, your progress is halted. Guilt and shame consume you, and it is a fight for you to once again face the sun. When we are consumed by darkness, it hurts to turn on the light. Our eyes have to once again become adjusted to that added light, and our progress is halted until we are once again acclimated to it.

If I could give people who are stuck in the survivor mindset one solid piece of advice when it comes to overcoming their shadows, it is this: Every time a problem or negative thought comes to your mind, write it down and then write down three solutions. You will find when you do this, your problems really aren't as big as your mind makes them out to be. This one simple solution can literally change your life. I know that's a bold claim, and using the phrase "change your life" is often overused, but test it out for even just a month to see for yourself.

We all have moments that help to define us. It isn't really these moments, though, that become the defining moments of our lives—it is our perception of these moments. It is the story we tell ourselves that propels us forward or sends us spiraling backwards. Do we head towards the sun, or do we turn back towards our shadow, consumed by our fears?

In order to progress, you must always choose to face the sun. Always move forward—even if you are crawling. Don't be a prisoner of your past.

Choose to follow the sun.

THE CONQUEROR MINDSET

I have not always had the conqueror mindset, and I continue to work on seeing life through the eyes of a conqueror. But I have had many experiences where I have been able to shift my mindset and conquer my fears. Serving a mission for my church was one of those life-changing experiences, especially when it came to fear of the unknown. I began my journey excited to face the unknown. But when things got tough, I was ready to go back to what was comfortable. It was painful being outside of my comfort zone. I had two choices: I could go back to what was comfortable and continue being just a survivor, or I could conquer my fears. I chose to conquer.

When I left to go serve a two-year church mission to do humanitarian work and spread the word of God to Argentina, I thought I was ready. I was so ready, that when I left to board the plane, my whole family was crying, but I was smiling. Sure, I was going to miss them, but I was excited to face the unknown that stretched out before me like an endless field of possibilities.

When I arrived in Argentina, the church leader in charge interviewed me. He asked me if I was homesick. With a grin I told him to send me wherever he wanted in Argentina and I will outwork anyone. I told him I wasn't homesick at all.

This was absolutely the case—at that moment. Most of the other missionaries with me at the time were very homesick. They were crying, out of either fear of the unknown, or missing their families. But I wasn't one of those kids. I was nineteen years old and ready to give back to the world.

My church leader laughed and sent me on my way. I was assigned to Tierra Del Fuego, which is the most southern city on this earth that is livable. It is the closest livable place to Antarctica—which I am sure is one of the coldest places on Earth. I tell you this to give you perspective on how cold it was, so you can understand my situation.

A year before I arrived, a missionary had died during the night due to a gas leak in the heater. Because of this, we were told not to use the heaters at night. Every night, I slept in a sleeping bag with a beanie. In the morning, I would shower in cold water. To make matters worse, the shower had no pressure. Imagine living in a place where the average temperature was already freezing cold, and then jumping into a cold shower with very little pressure. I promise you, it was not a pleasurable experience and it was completely outside of my comfort zone.

It gets worse. I didn't speak the language. I understood very little Spanish at that time. As a new missionary, I was partnered up with a more experienced missionary to train me in both the area as well as what to do. But the problem was that the other missionary was from Argentina and didn't speak any English. Again, I was well out of my comfort zone.

Even still, I kept thinking to myself that it would get better and that was my chance to make a difference in the world. I kept the story in my mind positive and moved forward, even though I felt like I was barely crawling.

I started knocking on doors with my trainer every day in the freezing cold weather, looking for people who needed any kind of help. Whether it was helping them build their house (just about everyone in Argentina builds their own house) or sharing a message about God—I was there to serve.

Despite my good intentions, people weren't interested in my message, nor did they want my help. We would walk all day and into the night knocking on doors. Some days, we were only let into homes once or twice. My feet were tired. My body was tired. My mind was tired. I was cold and weary and very, very uncomfortable.

Don't forget I was nineteen years old. I was in a foreign country where I didn't even speak the language. And I had come to the country to help people who didn't even want my help. I felt helpless. I felt useless. And because I couldn't properly communicate with anyone around me, I felt alone.

I became delusional and a month into my service, I literally hoped a car would hit me so that I could go back to America. I wouldn't even look when I crossed the street. I thought that if I was injured by a car, I would have to be sent back to America and wouldn't be considered a quitter because it was due to unfortunate circumstances. I wanted to go back to my comfort zone—to return to the country I was born in, speaking the language I grew up with.

I wasn't a victim of my circumstances, nor was I a conqueror. I was simply surviving.

It was the most depressing, hardest, and loneliest time of my life. I literally felt like each day I wasn't sure how I was going to get through that day. I know it sounds miserable and pretty dramatic. As difficult as it sounds, words can't do justice to describe how unhappy I was. This was the very first time I had felt any sort of depression in my life for more than an entire day. Even when my little brother died, I quickly found the positive.

I decided to take one day at a time. I didn't quit and I didn't make the choice to go home. I didn't have any one specific moment that changed everything. I just made a decision to stay in Argentina, learn a little more each day, and focus on taking it one day at a time. I decided to not dwell on some of the negative aspects of my life, but instead on the positives. I was living in a foreign country! I was seeing and experiencing a different culture. I had a roof over my head and warm clothes to wear. I maintained a positive attitude because after all, that's what I could control in those circumstances—me. After a few months, I became acclimated to my new surroundings. In other words, I chose to face the sun, and eventually I became acclimated to it. I stopped looking back and chose to move forward. I began to understand the language and ever so slowly, I started to feel useful.

Despite my feelings of uselessness earlier, I always worked as hard as I could. The fact that I kept moving forward, even when it was hard, is what transformed me from a survivor in the situation to a conqueror.

After my first four months, I finally felt like I had gone through the hardest times. I felt prepared to handle any trial. I became a workhorse and found great joy in serving others. As my attitude shifted, slowly the people in the area shifted and were willing to accept help. I spent the remainder of those two years 100 percent focused on the people that I served.

This experience was one of those experiences that has set a tone for my life. It gave me perspective on trials and the different mindsets we can use to approach those trials. I am so glad I listened to the right voice and didn't listen to the negative voices.

When it comes to fear of the unknown, the conqueror chooses to embrace the unknown and they value the good and the not-so-good in it. They use hard lessons to positively impact their future. They see the cup as neither half full nor half empty. They see the cup completely full—half is full of air and the other half full of water. This allows conquerors to focus on the possibilities that arise from a positive outcome, rather than focusing on all the negative things that could happen.

When the outcome of a certain choice is less than desirable, conquerors don't let it get them down or stop them from making future choices. They choose to see even negative outcome as a learning opportunity, and they use them as a measuring stick for future understanding and growth. They learn to be the author of their own story and they choose which story they are going to believe. And most importantly, conquerors find ways to keep moving forward, even when moving forward is hard and the outcome is unknown. Some days, they might be barely crawling, but even in their crawl, they recognize and value the progression.

I could have easily given up on what became one of the most life defining experiences of my life. But I didn't. I chose to live outside of my comfort zone, and not just live there, but thrive there. I didn't retreat back behind the barrier of what I knew; I embraced the unknown and lived there until it became known to me. And once the unknown became known, not only did it change my life—it became very precious to me.

I am here to encourage you to stop fearing the unknown and to become a conqueror when it comes to stepping outside of your comfort zone. One of the best things you can do in life is to courageously step into the unknown. Sure, it may be hard, and it may not always turn out for the best, but I can promise you that you will grow from it. And those experiences you have from embracing the unknown will be some of life's greatest rewards.

HOW TO CONQUER FEAR OF THE UNKNOWN

Ralph Waldo Emerson said this:

"When a resolute young fellow steps up to the great bully—the world—and takes him boldly by the beard, he is often surprised to find it comes off in his hand. It was only tied on to scare away the timid adventurers."

When you let go of your fear of the unknown, and address that fear, you are able to see things as they really are. And once you start taking steps into the unknown, greater things will be made known to you, until you realize it wasn't really scary after all.

Here are some ways to face the fear of the unknown, take it boldly by the beard, and become that conquering adventurer.

- **FACE YOUR FEAR.** If you are scared to step into the unknown, just do it! It really isn't as scary as you think. Our minds are so imaginative. Give up on imagining what could go wrong, and just go and see for yourself.

- **CHANGE YOUR WAY OF THINKING.** Rather than dwelling on the negative things that could happen from stepping into the unknown, write down and focus on all of the positive possibilities that can come from it. Make these your constant focus and allow them to create the motivation and hope you need to move forward.

- **TAKE SMALL STEPS.** Rather than making a big decision all at once, create baby steps that you can take instead. Ease into the decision one step at a time until you feel more comfortable with the choice. Give yourself a timeframe to complete each step so that you are not prolonging the decision or procrastinating. Each step needs to lead you closer to your destination and goal.

- **GET COMFORTABLE WITH BEING UNCOMFORTABLE.** It

has been said that there is no growth in the comfort zone, and no comfort in the growing zone. You can learn to get comfortable with discomfort by doing one thing every day that takes you outside of your comfort zone, whether that is talking to a stranger, making a phone call, or submitting a resume. If you make it a habit to regularly move outside of your comfort zone, discomfort actually becomes more comfortable to you.

- **FIND SOLUTIONS.** As I said before, you can find solutions for your fears, and discover great ways to overcome them by writing down each problem and brainstorming at least three solutions to that problem. Our brains may be hardwired to think those negative thoughts, but we are also hardwired to solve problems. Writing is a great way for our brain to process those negative thoughts and provide solutions. Let's get your brain to work for you and focus on solutions.

- **VISUALIZE CONQUERING.** Fear of the unknown often comes because we cannot see the future. In order to help overcome this, imagine, step by step, how you will move forward and conquer your problem. Visualize everything that could happen—even the scary things—and visualize how you will face those scary things and work through them. Once you have seen yourself conquering in your mind, you have less fear and apprehension moving forward because you have already seen the future and conquered it.

Facing the future isn't easy, especially if you have had a troubled past. But I can promise that if you make the effort to face your fears, you will find greater happiness and success. Once you have overcome your fear of the unknown, you can move forward in everything that you do with confidence. What sets a conqueror apart from the other mindsets is that whatever unknown they are faced with—they embrace it with open arms.

THE GAME OF CONQUERING

"The way out of judgement begins when you witness the judgement without more judgement."

-Gabrielle Bernstein

CHAPTER 10

JUDGED

instein.

The name alone is linked to genius. He said:

"Everybody is a genius. But if you judge a fish by its ability to climb a tree, it will live its whole life believing that it is stupid."

Judgment was persistent and often loud throughout Albert Einstein's entire life. He was labeled as slow in school. In college he had a terrible reputation for skipping class and not listening during lectures. He almost let the judgment of others squash his dream to get a college degree. At one point, he nearly gave up on his education to go and sell life insurance.

It wasn't just the world of education that judged him either. Albert's dad died with the judgment that his son would be a complete failure at life. But Albert never let the fear of judgment stop him from knowing what he was capable of.

Einstein said, "In the middle of every difficulty lies opportunity." The opportunity he saw in the face of judgment was that he was able to explore and stay curious, because no one expected anything except for stupidity from him.

I saved the fear of judgment as the last fear to discuss for a reason. The fear of judgment is the CORE of all other mental fears. The fear of judgment plays an important role in all other fears. I researched countless fears as I started to write this book. I analyzed how they impact the network marketing industry, and how the three different mindsets handled fears. The most common theme I came across during my research was the fear of judgment, as everything stems from it.

For instance, if we look at the fear of failure, we can see that we fail often. It is not the failure itself that we fear. It is the fear of people finding out about our failure. That is what our fear is truly based upon.

I want you to imagine trying something you have never done before. It can be anything. Now, I want you to imagine that no one else is around. How willing are you to try that new thing with no one around? How willing are you to fail and try again? How would this experience be different if you knew you couldn't fail?

The fear of judgment sometimes compels us to hide who we really are in order to avoid the negative judgment of others. We believe it is better to be invisible than to be judged negatively. We give more value to the opinions of others than to the value we hold for ourselves. We give up being who we are meant to be for fear of venturing outside of the social lines of what is appropriate. We never dare to live authentically.

Truth bomb here! No matter the circumstances, judgment is going to happen. We are a thinking, mentally alert people. We are all going to make judgments because it is in our very nature. It is how we base our decisions and how we learn through experience. But that doesn't mean you need to take someone else's judgment and adopt it into your view of yourself and allow it to become a part of your life.

Judgments are opinions based on the personal preferences of the person who is making the judgment. They have very little to do with the person being judged. Judgment most often is a reflection of the judger's own insecurities.

For example, we make judgments every morning about what to wear based on the weather or the activities we have planned. When we drive to work, we judge which path to take based on the traffic at the time. And when we eat, we judge the food we choose based on our personal preferences. What we choose and the opinions we make are most often determined according to our own personal preferences.

Judgments are also a way for humans to categorize and understand the world. When we make judgments, it helps us feel secure that we know what is going on around us and that we can be in control of the circumstances we are in. Judgments are usually made with only partial information. Our brain takes in the information it has and makes a judgment before it has ALL the information. Even if all the information proves the judgment to be incorrect, some may stick with it because our brain is partial to first impressions.

Fear of judgment keeps us from solving problems and creating solutions. It causes us to worry so much that something or everything we say or do may be seen negatively, we forget about our own strengths and ability to contribute. We keep our message to the world hidden for fear that our message will be rejected. Can you see how this shows up in your network marketing business? What would you be able to create and accomplish if you could drop the fear of judgment and authentically go all in?

The comments I often receive from people are these: "Rob, the company doesn't have great resources." "Rob, I am afraid of upsetting my upline doing the business my way." "Rob, I don't want to be seen as a slimy salesperson." Do these statements have anything in common? ABSOLUTELY. Each one of these people has a fear of being judged. They are using their fear to keep them from moving forward, solving problems, and being creative with solutions. They don't want to be judged by the company's resources, and they don't want to be judged by others. The fear of judgment presents itself as many different things, but like I said before, it is at the core of most fears.

In addition to this, the judgments we fear are simply our own thoughts projected onto someone else. We judge ourselves harshly, so we assume that others are judging us harshly, as well. We often speak to ourselves in negative words that we would never say to another person. In reality, it is often our own thoughts that betray us and cause us the most harm.

Looking at the fear of judgment through the different mindsets of the victim, survivor, and conqueror can be very enlightening. AND on top of that, understanding that fear of judgment is at the core of all fear in network marketing can have the power to shift our focus. Each mindset is going to experience judgment, but it is how they view that judgment that defines their thoughts and their actions.

Be mindful of others' points of view. One of my favorite quotes is "We judge others by their actions, we judge ourselves by our intentions."

At the beginning of the book, I called the fear of judgment the one fear to rule them all. The more research I did, the more I found this to be true. Failure is scary because we don't want others to perceive us as weak. Inadequacy is tough because it means that we aren't enough and will never be. Missing out feels terrible because we judge ourselves for not being able to be or do certain things. The unknown freaks us out because we don't even know what we will need to judge! The fear of judgment is the vein that runs through all fear.

When you can really understand how the fear of judgment plays a role in your life and the stories you tell yourself, that is where the real magic lies. That is where we can really start to gain awareness, get vulnerable, and take action from there.

THE VICTIM MINDSET

I have never told anyone this: I never had a "real" job until I was 23. I mean, I worked for my parents growing up, but I didn't actually work for anyone, or have a boss.

When I was 23, I was married, going to college, and on the tennis team. I decided it was time to start making some money to provide for my new family.

I was too scared to go out and apply for jobs, so I did what I do best—I started networking. A friend told me he had a job I could do. His company printed ads and marketing pieces for companies to hang on their door. My job was to get more clients for them.

I was supposed to make so many calls every day. Once again, instead of doing any cold calls, I inquired to see if anyone in my network needed this service. Lucky for me, one person did.

This job was paid solely on commission. I only got paid on what I sold.

Three weeks had gone by and I only had one client. I was still refusing to cold call because I was completely freaked out of my mind about cold calling people.

I was so embarrassed that I wouldn't do cold calls that I told my wife I just wasn't interested in that job anymore. I justified that it wasn't a great job, and the product wasn't needed or wanted by companies.

I felt like such a victim that I never told anyone about this job. I didn't want to be judged for my failure at my first job. As I am writing this book, my wife is reading it. She laughed and said, "I forgot that you had that job." I blocked it out of our lives and had skipped over it so much that my wife had even forgotten about it!

Because of fear of judgment, victims will try to solicit sympathy in an attempt to curb the negative judgments of others. When their weaknesses or past circumstances are exposed, victims will also make a list of excuses to explain away those circumstances and poor choices.

By making excuses, victims will blame other people or circumstances for their hardships in order to place themselves in a more positive light. But it's their excuses that keep them a victim, as they search for the sympathy of others. Excuses allow someone with the victim mindset to put responsibility outside themselves and take no control over their own lives.

I am not a stranger to the fear of judgment. And although I rarely solicit sympathy from others, when I was a teenager, I found myself making excuses for my circumstances. Whenever I would lose at tennis, I would make excuses for the loss. My victim mentality developed only after the fear of judgment came. We can become victims by the stories we choose to tell ourselves.

Victims never confront challenging circumstances because they worry that by speaking up, they will make other people feel uncomfortable. They will keep quiet and continue in a cycle of silence for the sake of keeping the people around them in a state of contentment. Victim mindset avoids making judgments as much as possible.

Victims see it as an admirable quality—and even at times, their duty— to keep the peace and go with the status quo. But in doing this, they forget they have a voice. They are so afraid to do or say anything because they fear they might trigger a negative response in someone else, so they end up not saying anything at all.

We all need to Stop Making Excuses! The greatest way we can overcome this victim mindset is to stop making excuses. You can make excuses, or you can make it happen. It's really that simple. We are creators, and we can either create our alibis of why we can't move forward, or we can create our conqueror story with the vision of how we can.

We can overcome any fear that life places before us—especially the fear of judgment. You and I have no control over the thoughts of other people. We can't make people agree with us or see things our way all the time. Their judgments are really none of our business. If we always concern ourselves with the judgment of others, we hold ourselves back and we are unable to achieve our full potential.

What we do have control over is ourselves. We can choose to not give into the fear of others and let go of the lies and excuses. We can control the thoughts and judgments we make of others. Compassion is the cure for judgment. Once we learn compassion—for ourselves and others—the fear of judgment goes out the window.

THE SURVIVOR MINDSET

This one may shock a ton of you. After working hard for five years, I was having great success in my business, and I had started to do some public speaking. Despite all the success, there wasn't ONE post on social media about me doing public speaking OR anything about my business.

The main reason was that I was fearful of what other people thought. I was fearful about how people perceived me. I was afraid of being seen as an imposter. I didn't want people outside of my network marketing business to see me as a "fake business" person. I wanted to be liked by all. So, I kept quiet on social media, trying to hide from the judgment of others.

I knew plenty of people would judge me for leaving the tennis club, which I did when I left for network marketing. I had friends, family, and clients all questioning why I would leave a great position. Some even begged me to stay.

I was showing up for myself and following through with my goals despite what others thought But, on the other side, I feared letting people know what I was actually doing. I stayed quiet about what I was doing instead of running the tennis club. I decided the best thing to do was to survive others' opinions by not giving them any information on which to judge me.

Sometimes, I am quiet on purpose because I let my fear of judgment get in my own way. I let it hold me back from showing up as my authentic self and connecting with others. This is a fear that creeps its way into my life periodically. I am always working on adjusting and changing my mindset so that I don't let the fear of judgment hold me back on creating the life I want to live.

The truth is, there is judgment everywhere. It's just a part of life. Go and look up the reviews of your favorite book. You will see negative reviews. That is just part of putting yourself out there.

Recently, I spoke to a big crowd and they all gave me a rating after my presentation. I make it a habit to look at ALL of the reviews and feedback. I got a 9.1 out of 10. I wanted to read all the comments and see what people said. Here are some of the comments from the low reviews: "Way too monotone." "Absolutely boring." "Rob, seems like he was on another planet and NEVER landed." Right away, when I read those reviews the fear of judgment came to me.

I hate when people don't like me. But I have learned how to deal with it. I have made it a strength of mine to care about other people, and I can take how they perceive me into consideration but won't let it consume me.

It hurt, but I had to put it in perspective. The more success that you have, the more criticism and "haters" you are going to have. I had to see all the comments and feedback as a place to gain knowledge of areas I need to grow and work on. I also had to remind myself that other people's opinions are just that—opinions.

Even still, it doesn't feel good. I had to go back and have a talk with myself. It was a personal development moment for me. "Look, this is part of life. This is part of the journey. Your goal is to be the BOLD version of yourself."

Survivors strive to leave their past behind them—hidden under a pile of their own greatness. They don't want to expose their vulnerability, and they desire to be seen as someone who has it all together. The fear of judgment is always in their minds, and many of their actions are based on getting judged in a positive way.

Another way survivors deal with the fear of judgment is with defensiveness. Survivors already judge themselves harshly, but when they face other people's judgments that are exactly the same as their own, they often get defensive. They don't want others to see their weaknesses and don't want to admit to others the judgments they themselves are personally battling inside their own minds.

Many times, survivors are so busy trying to play catch-up from their past that they can't focus on anything else. In the past, they felt they had no voice, and they no longer want to be perceived as weak in that regard. They have swung the pendulum all the way to the other end of the spectrum. They make it a point to speak up and speak out often, without regard to the feelings of others. They are so busy trying to cover up their own insecurities and need for perfection that they don't recognize the needs of others.

Oftentimes, they will put others down in order to help themselves feel better about their own life and choices. Survivors simply tell themselves and others they are right, and they don't back down. Their justification prevents them from moving forward. They are so consumed with justifying, and trying to be seen as right, that they can't see where they are wrong and adjust. They can't admit they are wrong because that perfect image will be shattered. To the survivor, that would be the ultimate defeat. Their pride would be wounded, and they would have to admit and be seen as imperfect.

Many times with the survivor mindset, we are too insecure and lack the maturity to really assess our decisions. Our lack of assessing and challenging our decisions prevents us from conquering our fears. It prevents us from progress. It prevents us from success.

THE CONQUEROR MINDSET

Before I said yes to any network marketing business, I had over eleven network marketing companies approach me about joining, and I said no to every single one. It wasn't that their product or offer wasn't great. I even loved some of their compensation plans. I said no because of fear of judgment from others. I was so worried about what other people thought.

The state that I live in has the largest amount of network marketing companies operating (per capita) than any other place in the world. It seems like everyone is either doing network marketing, failed at network marketing, or has a sister or a friend in network marketing. My belief was that there was more judgment, and there were more people with a negative experience with network marketing here than any other place. I always felt like people would look down on me if I was "that guy" with a network marketing business.

When I finally said yes to my first networking marketing business, I still had the fear of judgment. One of my neighbors found out about my business and started to make fun of me for it. On the outside I acted as if I didn't care, but on the inside, I cared a lot. I used that as evidence that the fear was real and tried to keep my business quiet from my group of social influence. When people asked what I did for a living, I found every creative way to not directly answer the question. Having a conqueror's mindset around telling people about my network marketing business didn't happen overnight. It was a process.

Within my network marketing business, I was scared to tell people that I never had a sip of alcohol or smoked anything. I was scared to share that I avoid R-Rated movies and that I do my best to avoid working on Sundays. I felt that by sharing these things, many would either laugh at me or think I was some crazy person that judged everyone else. The fear of judgment is in all of us. I used to be scared to share who I was, who I am, and who I want to be.

Then it HIT me—STOP trying to be someone else—BE YOU. I had heard it a million times, but it never really set in. I realized that what other people think of me doesn't matter. I know I don't think I'm better than any other person. And I know I don't judge someone for choosing to live their life differently than me.

I knew my intentions but was so worried about how others would perceive and judge my intentions. Now—I constantly share me—and my story. I share my strengths and my weaknesses. I share my learning lessons and obstacles. I'll be honest, I still don't talk a lot of business in social settings. But the reasons have completely changed. I like to keep the two areas separate. I am committed to being present with friends and leave business for work time.

The conqueror uses judgments to improve and grow. They realize that what other people think about them is not their number one concern and isn't the driving force behind their actions. But instead, when negative opinions are given and judgments made, they look for lessons in the critiques, use them to improve themselves, and continue moving forward. If there is no value in the judgment, they simply let it go. The judgments and opinions of others have little to no effect on a conqueror's sense of worth or the view they have of themselves.

Conquerors also use their difficult experiences and past choices to move them forward. Rather than burying their past, they find the good in their hardships and seek to share that good with others. Their mess becomes their message. Their test becomes their testimony. Their struggle becomes the most powerful part of their story because they have learned to overcome it. And because of this, they can do much good in the world.

Most of us are people pleasers by nature, and I am no different. I often joke that I am a recovering people pleaser. When I first started public speaking, I would always find ways to try and be agreeable with others. I was scared to mention my beliefs in God in any of my presentations for years. My fear was that I would lose some of my audience if I opened up and revealed who I really was.

In challenging times, and when making difficult decisions, those who succeed are often the ones who rely on their intuition, which is not influenced by outside forces. It won't be easy to go against what is popular, but you have to stop worrying about what everyone else thinks.

One of the best ways to have success as a conqueror is to focus. NICHES TO RICHES. Stop trying to be everything to everyone. Find your tribe—those who love you for being you. Those are the people you surround yourself with. There are so many different ways to success; but one of the fastest ways to failure is trying to please everyone. Because you never will.

Stop being fake. It doesn't feel great and doesn't create real relationships or happiness. Why do we work so hard in gaining the approval of others? If you aren't your true self and you gain someone's approval, it is FAKE! It is a facade.

Relationships are one of the greatest indicators for true happiness. When we build fake relationships through our fake actions, we are building our happiness with no real foundation. But good relationships are strengthened when we risk judgment—when we are willing to open ourselves up and disclose who we really are, regardless of our fears of the outcome.

Being the best version of you starts with YOU becoming comfortable with who you are and who you are becoming. This means that you have to stop listening to what other people say about you. What others say doesn't really matter. You have to believe in you and place your belief in yourself as greater than the hurtful judgments that will surely come your way. Know your worth and let those negative judgments fall away.

Look—that doesn't mean that you think you are perfect, but you own who you are. We all have tons of room for improvement, but beating yourself up for past mistakes and current weaknesses will not do any good. Neither will hiding past mistakes or weaknesses under a facade of perfection. Focus on the present. What are you going to do today to progress your life forward?

And most important of all—stop making yourself smaller to make others feel comfortable. Be your very best and you unknowingly will inspire others to become a better version of themselves, as well. Lift others up. Don't let others pull you down.

Let the judgments come and make peace with them. Recognize their source, thank them for their opinion, learn the lessons you can from them, then discard them and move on. Life is too short to allow other people's judgments to determine your actions. You are in the driver's seat of your own life's journey. Don't allow anyone else to take the wheel and decide where you are going to go. It is your life. Live it! You are the best person in the world to do you.

That is how we conquer—we first have to be willing to try, even if others laugh at us and make us feel small. People can only make us feel small if we let them. We have to see our greatness, especially when others can't. If we try and fail, simply recognize the failure and allow it to propel you forward. It doesn't matter what other people think of the failure or even what they think of you. Learn from it and move on. That is the only way we can overcome the fear of judgment. We have to believe in ourselves and see our own potential. We have to be willing to act—even when acting is hard—and not let anyone or anything hold us back.

HOW TO CONQUER FEAR OF JUDGMENT

Because we live in a world with more than a billion other people with their own ideas and opinions, we will never be able to live a life free from judgment. But that's okay, because once we learn to face this fear and conquer it, those judgments will no longer hold us back. We will be able to move forward boldly and courageously with a determination to succeed.

If this fear is one you struggle with, here are some tips that may help you overcome it. As I have overcome my own fear of judgment, these tips have been a valuable resource for me.

- **DON'T LET OTHERS DEFINE YOU.** There will always be someone there to share their opinion on how you should live your life. Practice saying, "Thank you for your opinion. I appreciate it. But I think I am going to do this the way. I feel inspired to do it." Then go out there and do it without any regrets.

- **BE THE BOLD AUTHENTIC YOU.** Never pretend to be someone you are not in order to impress someone else. No matter what kind of relationship it is, if they don't like you for you, you are not a good fit for each other. Let go and move on.

- **KNOW WHO YOU ARE.** Create a mission statement of who you are and who you are striving to become. Outline your beliefs, motivations, and values. If anyone ever challenges who you are, or your motivations behind doing something, refer to that mission statement. It will help you remember who you are and remind you of where you are going. Read it out loud daily. Share with others frequently

- **VALUE WHO YOU ARE AND YOUR CONTRIBUTION.** If you recognize and know your value, others will too. Keep a list of your experiences, accomplishments, and goals to review often, especially when you are feeling like a failure because of someone else's judgment. We are all worthy in this world and we all have value that we can contribute to it. Find others you look up to, who share your beliefs, and befriend them. They can become a great support to you in your efforts to share who you are. Not only will they be an advocate for you, but they will help you remember that you are not alone in your beliefs. This can be a great confidence booster. As you share your opinions with these trusted individuals, don't forget the value of listening. Listen to these valued leaders, which will help give you even more insight.

- **FIND YOUR PLACE OF PEACE.** Create positive affirmations and repeat them to yourself in the mirror each morning. When someone questions you and judgments are made, repeat these affirmations to yourself. Let your positive voice of reinforcement drown out others' negativity.

- **BE KIND TO YOURSELF.** Sometimes it is our own judgments of ourselves that become our downfall. Be aware of your inner-critic and when that critical voice starts to rear its ugly head. Practice positive self-talk. Take time every day to talk to yourself before you talk to anyone else. So many of us have huge EGOs and laugh at this idea of positive self-talk. Take some time reminding yourself of who you are and why your voice is important. Use positive affirmations in your morning routine that help keep you in a positive state of mind. Once you are in a good place, it will be easier for you to share your voice, and more people will be receptive to what you have to say. Morning routines set the tone for the day.

- **OBTAIN INTERNAL VS EXTERNAL VALIDATION.** My good friend, Woody Woodward, is an expert on internal thoughts vs external thoughts. Internal validation is seeking approval from self, while external validation is seeking approval from others. He explains the following differences in outcomes from external vs internal validation:

LONG-TERM RESULTS FROM EXTERNAL VALIDATION

Envy	Sorrow	Jealousy
Anger	Fear	Fatigue
Overwhelmed	Sadness	Exhaustion
Pride	Loneliness	Loss
Ego	Disappointment	Overloaded
Frustration	Covetous	Backbiting
Gossip	Incomplete	Hatred
Scarcity	Entropy	

LONG-TERM RESULTS FROM INTERNAL VALIDATION

Peace	Happiness	Confidence
Energy	Patience	Love
Meekness	Humility	Strength
Power	Leadership	Productivity
Charity	Longsuffering	Hopeful
Faith	Abundant	Clarity
Hope	Insight	Longevity
Control	Forgiveness	

I can promise you that the more you strive to conquer this fear, the more confidence you will have to take action in your life. You will have the incredible ability to do all those things in life that will bring you greater success and an abundance of happiness. All these ideas are great—but if you know everything and do nothing—you know nothing. So, go out there and conquer!

"I learned that courage was not the absence of fear, but the triumph over it. The brave man is not he who does not feel afraid, but he who conquers that fear."

-Nelson Mandela

CONCLUSION

Anyone can do this business. I have seen people of all walks of life have success in this business. I have seen people who have never had success in any other area of their life come into network marketing and create success.

I remember how much I used to be afraid of public speaking. When I was a teenager, I watched my dad once speak in front of a group of people and thought, "That is the absolute scariest thing ever." Talking to strangers also seemed scary and daunting to me.

That is why network marketing always felt like a big NO for me. I would have to conquer all my fears in order to be successful. As I look back and reflect on the person I was, and the person I am now, I am so grateful for this industry. I was the kid that wouldn't speak in church. The kid who wouldn't get up and swing a baseball bat in front of people. The kid who was naturally the shy introvert. I am grateful for the chances I had to face my fears in different mindsets and be able to

THE GAME OF CONQUERING

see the difference it makes to be willing to shift, learn, and grow from my experiences.

Victims focus on the past.

Survivors focus too much on the future.

Conquerors learn from the past and have a vision for the future but focus on the present.

Conquering fear requires courage and the ability to think intentionally and act in a positive, constructive way. It requires you to break old habits and end destructive cycles that are keeping you bound to your negative circumstances. And it requires a new way of viewing yourself, the world, and those around you. You can fight the negative effects of fear through your own positive thoughts and actions.

Jim Rohn said:

"You must take personal responsibility. You cannot change the circumstances, the seasons, or the wind, but you can change yourself. That is something you have charge of."

The greatest way to conquer your fears and overcome a difficult situation is to change yourself. Sincerely ask yourself the question, "What can I do to conquer my fear and move forward in my desires?" Take responsibility and make it happen for yourself. You will be amazed at how your circumstances change once you take personal responsibility for your life and start living in the conqueror's mindset. There is so much you can change when you start taking charge of yourself, your thoughts, and your actions.

As you seek to break old cycles and learn new habits, make it a habit to treat yourself kindly. This is a process, and it doesn't happen overnight. The first step is to find the places that you are judging yourself. Stop the negative self-talk and replace it with positive, uplifting thoughts about yourself. Confidence in yourself is a foundational step in overcoming fear and creating the life you dream of. Understand who you are and the value you bring to the world and then share who you are with others.

Oftentimes, we shrink back. We believe it is prideful to believe in ourselves and value who we are. I love what I learned from Jim Rohn. He taught that putting yourself down isn't humble. He then shared that when someone said to Jesus Christ, "You are the Son of God," Jesus didn't deny it. Of course, Jesus did not say, "Oh, no, I am not. You are way too kind." No! Jesus knew who he was and didn't deny it. He lived an authentic life. Likewise, don't deny who you are and the power within you to make lasting change. Live authentically.

Don't make your dreams, goals, and ambitions small to appease others. Don't put your achievements down to make others feel more comfortable. I am giving your permission today to step into your greatness! Give that permission to yourself.

When we are younger, we typically dream big, believing we can become anything in life. As we grow older, and life hits us upside the head with challenges, we stop getting our hopes up because we don't want to be let down. We stop dreaming big. We start to shrink our dreams and aspirations because WE THINK it is easier to think small so that we are never let down—so that we never feel the pain of failure.

But it is vital for us to understand that everything worthwhile is HARD. The game of conquering is not an easy game. Life can be hard. Being married is hard. Being single is hard. Having kids is hard. Not having kids is hard. Having a job is hard. Not having a job is hard. Life is perceived as hard, but it is your perception of hard that matters. It is the mental battle that we all deal with that defines our true state. What mindset are you bringing into battle with you?

You are the narrator of your own story. You can choose to narrate your own experiences as failures or learning lessons. You can choose to narrate your life as a victim, a survivor, or a conqueror. It is my sincere hope that this book helps you to navigate life as a conqueror.

In conclusion, I would like to share one last story of how I overcome my fears. I also want to issue you a challenge.

I shared with you early in this book what I wrote in my phone when I first started my network marketing journey:

"I have never tried to go all out and do something completely different because I am always scared of failing. I will go forward no matter what. When I get rejected, I will just become more determined. This is my break and opportunity. I deserve this right now."

I read this statement out loud five to ten times a day and it helped me have the determination to move forward.

As you know by now, I am an introvert, but I am an ambitious one. My fears are high, but many times my ambitions are even higher. It is always a battle between my fears and my ambitions. My fears have a voice and my ambitions have a voice. We all have those inner voices, and we have to decide who is going to win.

When it comes to those inner voices, I believe that one voice is from God, or whatever higher being you believe in, while the other voice is from the adversary. One voice wants you to become the person you are meant to become. The other voice is purposely telling you that you aren't good enough, worthy enough, smart enough, or strong enough.

I see so many people who think that being the survivor is enough. And I am here to give you some tough love and tell you that it isn't enough. I have been there. I was the person who was just surviving in network marketing. I do not believe God sent us down to this earth to be average. The adversary is placing doubt in every mind. The adversary doesn't want us to reach our potential. He wants us to stay average. In fact, he wants us to be less than average. He uses subtleties—whispering thoughts into our minds—making us believe they are our own. He whispers things like, "Don't even attempt to do this, because people may laugh at you." By doing this, he leads us down the path of becoming, or staying, a victim—the path of mediocrity. My advice to you today, and forever more, is to stop listening to him.

I am still learning. I am still doing. I am still overcoming. I am still seeking to be the conqueror in my own life. On a daily basis I am trying to become the conqueror. It's a journey. I still have days or moments of being the survivor or victim. But I get out of the moments faster. Learning about mindsets and how they come into play in my own life has been a HUGE blessing for me. I hope this helps you become more self-aware. And not in a way that makes you feel guilty, but more that it creates progress and helps you become the conqueror that you are meant to become.

Remember what I asked you to do at the beginning of this book? I asked you to write down how you have shown up as a victim, survivor, and conqueror through each of the fears. Did you do it? What about the Conqueror's Formula? Do you remember it, and have you started to implement its teachings?

Grab the notebook, phone, or scrap of paper on which you jotted those experiences down. I want you to now write down your vision statement, your commitment statement, or your why for your life. I challenge you to write down something that you can read aloud several times a day. I challenge you to write something so powerful that when you read it OUT LOUD daily, it will help you listen to the right voice—YOUR voice.

With this statement, I now want you to go back to your stories. How does your statement help you start to see how these experiences can

ALL be changed to turn you into the conqueror of your life? When I started the work to have a conqueror's mindset, I did this same exercise to every single story I shared with you. As a conqueror, I can tell you that I am grateful for the experiences that I have had in my life. They have shaped me into the man I am today.

It is my sincere hope that as you read this book, you have found the courage to start the process to conquer your fears. I don't want you to just PLAY the game of conquering, I want you to WIN! We are all going to feel afraid at some point in our lives—and some may face fear every single day. But the brave man or woman is not the one who has no fear, but the one who stares that fear in the face with a conquering spirit.

One of the most simple and helpful things a reader can do for an author is to leave a book review. For more free resources don't forget to go to **www.sperrybonus.com**.

GO TO WWW.SPERRYBONUS.COM

FOR FREE TRAININGS.

A few of those trainings are:

- The Income Producing Activities

- Your Daily Method of Operation

- The Conqueror's Formula

- Public Speaking Tips

- Free eBook: *From One to a Thousand*